Behind The Scream
The Truth About Horror Films

By
Christopher Gregory

All Scripture quotations are taken from the King James Version of the Holy Bible. Unless otherwise noted, all photos used in the writing of Behind The Scream, The Truth About Horror Films, are the copyrighted properties of their original owners and subject to the laws of their initial Country. All photos are used under 17 USC 107 Limitations on exclusive rights: Fair use. The Author makes no claim to said ownership to any or all images contained in this Title.

Behind the Scream. The Truth About Horror Films
ISBN-13:978-1480057258   ISBN-10:1480057258
Printed in the United States of America
©2012 Christopher Gregory

Table of Contents

Preface...4

Chapter One: Horror 101...6

Chapter Two: A History of Horror......................................9

Chapter Three: Bram Stoker...20

Chapter Four: Seduction of Evil.......................................23

Chapter Five: Sex and Nudity in Horror...........................27

Chapter Six: The British are Coming................................29

Chapter Seven: Cause and Affect......................................35

Chapter Eight: The Late, Late Show.................................49

Chapter Nine: Saturday Morning Poison...........................54

Chapter Ten: Rocky's Perverted Horror Show...................62

Chapter Eleven: Creators of Evil Things...........................67

Chapter Twelve: Vampire Lesbianism...............................81

Chapter Thirteen: The Halloween Connection....................85

Chapter Fourteen: Slasher Films.......................................94

Chapter Fifteen: The Harry Potter Affect..........................100

Chapter Sixteen: A Christian Response to Evil...................105

Final Thoughts: 108

Preface

When I first considered writing "Behind the Scream", I was initially compelled by how much horror films had changed throughout the years. From the early years of simplistic cinema, to the more current age of digital CGI, horror films have morphed into something more than just a motion picture, it was turning into a cult following.

With my own background in the industry, I realized that what I was associating with and condoning was actually doing great harm, not only to others, but to my own spiritual health. Growing up for me at least, horror films were a bonding tool with me and my Father. Like others growing up in the 70s, television didn't have the sort of entertainment it does today, far from it. Limited channels, no cable at that specific time because cable had not yet been made available to the general public, we, like most Americans, got all of our channels thru the trusted set of rabbit ears that dominated the top of our old Zenith television.

Although I and my Father never talked much, our few conversations as Father and son were limited to the occasional greeting and my excuse as to why the chores were not done, and yes, during this era of early years, kids did have chores.

Yet the one thing we *did* have in common was horror films. It was, as strange as it may seem, the one common denominator which held the Father/son unit together. It was during this pivotal time in my life that horror films left a remarkable imprint upon my life which, to some extent, has remained through my adult years.

There is no good which can come from horror, only bondage. The allure, the mystical and soothing image it gives to many is like a song from a Banshee, hypnotizing those with her deathly melody. Like the Banshee, horror films represent a method which takes its victims and begins to undermine and condition their hearts as well as minds to Satanic influence. Horror films have done more to condition people, especially young people, to accept what normally would never be acceptable, to embrace what was once considered revolting and desire that which was once considered undesirable.

My objective in writing this book is to give parents the basic understanding of what horror films are, how they were created, *why* they were created and ultimately, how horror films have changed an entire society and its culture. The second part of that reasoning in writing this book is to explain to young people how they are being manipulate and ultimately used on a global scale to accept something which is wrong both morally as well as spiritually. Yes, horror films are wrong because they were invented by men with power to corrupt an entire culture, which was their initial agenda, their second agenda was to condition people into a mind set which suggested that the occult was to be accepted and Christianity rejected. That's the key - how horror films, for the most part, reflect an idea concerning Christianity.

If you want to know how true Christianity is viewed or considered by many in the film industry as well as literary, all one needs to do is look to horror. Is it any great wonder why writers like Stephen King or Anne Rice hates traditional Christianity? Is there an agenda going on toward Christianity itself by many in the entertainment and literary world? A futuristic agenda by many such as Aleister Crowley or the Studios themselves who, for the most part, combined their resources to undermine Christianity by imposing another form of ideology, based on occult themes such as Satanism? The answer is yes, there was and still is a plot to condition and manipulate generations of young people into a world system where Christianity is considered foolish, deluded and obsolete and another form of religion, one which is self centered and a promoter of evil things, worshiped.

We need to understand that the enemy is using everything in his arsenal to destroy our society and the lives which come across his path, but if we're ignorant to his weapons, if we look away and suggest that some of those weapons are innocent, or, in this case, "just a movie" then we've lost the battle before we even go to war. Satan is not shy about his hatred for modern man, he's made that perfectly clear ever since the garden, what we must do is understand his hatred and confront it, not with human efforts, but with the word as well as information based on spiritual enlightenment through his Holy Spirit.

It is this reason why I've written "Behind the Scream", so that all may see the ploys and tactics the enemy uses to deceive many in these last days.

Chapter One
Horror 101

Fear:
a distressing emotion aroused by impending danger, evil, pain, etc., whether the threat is real or imagined; the feeling or condition of being afraid. Synonyms: foreboding, apprehension, consternation, dismay, dread, terror, fright, panic, horror, trepidation, qualm. Antonyms: courage, security, calm, intrepidity.

There are two, distinct forces working in this present world - the spirit of God and the spirit of Satan and both can be felt around the world. In this present world there is a hidden, more darker ruler ship and that ruler who controls much, if not all, of this world's system is Satan himself. He is the God of this world and his impact can be felt all around us - especially in the world of entertainment.

There are characteristics of the enemy and the darkness he brings upon this world that captures seduces and ultimately controls or oppresses the people who are involved in this world, even Christians. There are many ways the enemy has affected those within this world and what he uses to affect the person or system, such as lust, envy, greed, hate, evil, depression and even deception. However, there is one particular spirit which Satan uses and uses very well which is the spirit of fear.

One could literally write an entire book on the aspects of fear and how the enemy uses such within this world. Satan uses fear in many aspects of our culture, from politics (the fear of the economy and direction of the Government) to world events (9-11, the middle east) and even the fear of war. But if I could narrow it down a bit, there is one aspect in which Satan has successfully used fear and created a system around the spirit of fear, and that is in the realm of horror films.

Fear is a powerful force when applied successfully. Unlike other emotions, nothing hinders or puts a person into a terror state like fear can. This is why fear, when used effectively, can actually cause a person to worry, lose sleep, have their life literally taken over by the power of the enemy to such a degree that they will lose all hope.

The success of horror films within our culture has been a long one. From the early 1920's to present, it's main objective has been to scare individuals, bringing about an emotional reaction for profit. The bottom line to the creation of movies or even books when it comes to the world of horror is it's all about money. The money used from the spirit of fear upon people has generated millions, if not billions in the Hollywood film industry.

Horror films have, for over 100 years, become apart of our culture. The rush one receives while sitting in a movie theater filled with people, the smell of fresh popped buttery popcorn, the rustling of candy paper, they all play a part on our senses when one sits and waits for the feature film to begin.

A Deception Revealed

A teaching usually leads to a belief.   When beliefs do not coincide with the facts someone has been misled and is living a lie.   Many have been taught that most, if not all, of what is being passed as "entertainment", in this case horror films, are harmless fun. We are taught in Government controlled schools, in social settings and in print (books, magazines) that we have Freedom and that freedom extends to us the luxury to enjoy those things which are exciting, adventurous - fun. That teaching is augmented by an influential means called, "Advertising".

Satan knows how to advertise better than any marketing firm in New York. Actually, if one were to notice how marketing and advertising, when it comes to horror movies, are made to bring people into the movie house, one will see a pattern of deception, from the moment of the commercial to the teaser trailers found just before the main feature, advertising is another form of manipulation to bring about a persons conditioning to accept something which is not good. This is called mind control.

Revelation 12:9; And the great dragon was cast out, that old serpent, called the Devil, and Satan, which deceiveth the whole world: he was cast out into the earth, and his angels were cast out with him.

John wrote the Book of Revelation 2,000 years ago.   John's choice or words reflect people in his time had been deceived and were living a lie.   That lie continues to be taught today.

Deception is synonymous with a lie.

II Corinthians 4:4; In whom the god of this world hath blinded the minds of them which believe not, lest the light of the glorious gospel of Christ, who is the image of God, should shine unto them.

The act of blinding someone's mind is bestowing lies upon them making them live and teach or preach those lies to future generations.

John 8:44; Ye are of your father the devil, and the lusts of your father ye will do. He was a murderer from the beginning, and abode not in the truth, because there is no truth in him. When he speaketh a lie, he speaketh of his own: for he is a liar, and the father of it.

II Corinthians 4:4 tells us specifically that Satanic forces control the earth.   This explains why the facts show we live in a Grand Illusion that includes a Societal Hierarchy of Control, Knowledge deprivation and Liberty deprivation. This is why the power and influence of the modern horror film is not just mere entertainment, but it's to condition the person to accept what they were initially built and designed to resist from their basic building blocks of God's DNA.

Horror films break down that wall of separation; they remove all thought of morals and values and replace them with images and ideas which reflect a more occult spiritual concept, rebellion, idol worship and human suffering. These are the traits of the modern horror film.

Have you noticed more and more violence in horror movies lately? Have you noticed more and more sexual content in horror films? Have you noticed the use of even children in many of the films being put out by many Studios who produced horror films? Why? Why is our culture, much less other parts of the world, beginning to accept and embrace violence and Satanic influence in this current hour? The answer is because society as well as the rest of the world is becoming more and more intolerant to anything remotely connected to Christianity.

There is what I call an "end time's celebration" of paganism, idolatry as well as occultism running rampant within our culture like never before in the history of the 20th century, and even now in the beginning of the 21st century. It seems wherever we turn, there is evil all around us. Violence seems to be prevalent in every aspect of our culture. Satan worship, even in the form of Vampires and Witches have become a staple in our society to the point where the darkest ideas are embraced and the best ideas, found in the teachings of Christ and his Holy word are rejected. That is why one will never find a horror film or television show that is based on the occult, sympathetic to the Christian faith, it is actually hostile to that belief system, and this is why horror films and the lives of Christians are incompatible with each other.

One of the final signs suggesting that we are in the last days is a reference to Noah found in Matthew 24:36-39; Luke 17:26-27 by Jesus himself. Christ warned us that in the final years just prior to his return, there would be a prevalence of wickedness and great evil, just as it was in the time of Noah. In our day, it's interesting to note that when cinema was beginning, the horror film was mild, yet greatly promoting the Satanic agenda. Yet, with every other aspect of technology, time would have to allow itself space to grow, allow technology to catch up with the inner visions and imaginations of those who were waiting to release their idea of Satanic agenda upon the world and condition millions into the occult, preparing many for the greater deception which is still to come.

Chapter Two
A History of Horror

HORROR
• noun 1) an intense feeling of fear, shock, or disgust. 2) a thing causing such a feeling. 3) intense dismay. 4) informal a bad or mischievous person, especially a child.
— ORIGIN Latin, from horrere 'shudder, (of hair) stand on end'.

There were not always horror films. Horror films are only about 200 years old. Before that, the only way a person could get their "fright on" was either through late night storytelling round the ancient fires of our ancestors, or, the most common way, in a book. From Mary Shelly's "Frankenstein", Edgar Allen Poe's "The Raven" or the ever popular - "Dracula" by Bram Stoker, the influence and power of horror has been around for centuries.

The first accepted horror film was in 1896 with George Melies' "Le Manoir de Diable - The Devil's Castle", it is also arguably the first vampire film of beginning cinema. Melies, a well known magician by his own right, was fascinated by the occult, black magic and Satanism. Melies began a complete work of occult themed horror film shorts throughout the early 1900's, all of which focused on Satanism, the occult, witchcraft and vampirism. It is believed that he, along with occultist Aleister Crowley, began the influence of others in this early beginning work with film and occultism.

With the success of Melies work, more ambitious and creative films began to emerge, but the one which seems, even to this day, and garnered more success is Tod Browning's "Dracula", featuring Hungarian born actor Bela Lugosi. No other film to this day sparks such admiration as Browning's film and, it should be noted, put Universal Pictures on the map when it came to horror cult classics. Even today, the monsters of Universal have become a permanent fixture in our society.

As "Dracula" gained more popularity with movie fans, other studios began the push with horror, "Frankenstein, The Wolf man, The Mummy" were just a few of the growing titles of ghastly characters of the undead that began to overtake cinema. The concept of horror films and their ability to create an assured source of revenue was the driving force behind producer's desire to green light and exploit this new market of simple entertainment. But was or is it just simple entertainment?

From the early beginnings of low budget horror to big budget blockbusters, horror films have literally outlasted every other genre in the movie industry, no other genre, whether it is action, westerns, drama, none has had the staying power or even influence upon a culture or society has that of the modern horror film. It's interesting to note that Thomas Edison, the creator of the modern day telephone was in fact the first American who created and produced the 1910 classic "Frankenstein", not to be confused with the later, 1930's Boris Karloff classic film.

Every aspect of filmmaking, from effects, design and creative writing owes much of its success to the horror film, thus making this wildly popular aspect of modern culture of eerie storytelling king above all others. Certainly it can be said that from a mere financial standpoint that the horror film was a guaranteed money maker for all involved against the instability of the world markets, however, what most who were involved in this genre did not understand is, there was and still is, a spiritual connection to this medium which not only enabled it's success, but it was influenced by those who lived in that spiritual world themselves - the prophets of Satanism.

One of those "Prophets" of such mysticism and occult influence in horror films was Aleister Crowley.

Edward Aleister Crowley was born in 1875, Warwickshire England. A student at Cambridge, Crowley began his study of the occult and mysticism at an early age. In 1898, Crowley was initiated in the secret order called the Hermetic Order of the Golden Dawn. This order was the beginning stage for what would become the imprint of demonic influence upon Crowley and eventually his influence upon those who would produce and create horror films for the marketplace.

One of those whom Crowley influenced with his teachings of the occult was novelist Dennis Wheatley. Wheatley penned such titles as, The Forbidden Territory, The Devil Rides Out and To The Devil - A Daughter, all of which would become successful horror films through Hammer Studios (London). Wheatley's interest in witchcraft, occult, black magic and sorcery would be interwoven in each book, characters whose influence came from a supernatural source (namely the occult) and whose adaptations were all based on Wheatley's own personal perspective on Satanism. It has been said that Wheatley owes much of his knowledge of Crowley, whom both met and had lunch while discussing their occultist views.

The power and influence of the supernatural within horror films have established a pattern which both celebrates as well as indoctrinates key aspects of forbidden science, the science of the occult. The global success of Harry Potter only proves this fact, even though, technically, Harry Potter is not a "horror film" in general terms, the trilogy as well as the literature from where it derived its roots were in fact based, or rooted from occult foundations, namely witchcraft. Yet horror films, like Harry Potter, can claim equal success simply due to the power and influence of its own occultist roots.

Witchcraft and necromancy has played a major role in most, if not all of the films created, of course the argument among many is, it's only reasonable since the very films themselves would be meaningless to watch if they did not contain at least one aspect of occult influence within its framework. That said, as we begin to trace more of the ancient roots of paganism as well as Satanism in the framework of most modern day horror films, we begin to see an overall pattern which not only directs the movie goers into a world of forbidden knowledge, it also brings with it a spiritual influence which can, when given enough access, begin to attach itself upon the person who allows themselves to be influenced by such forces.

Another individual in the world of the occult who had a profound influence on many within the horror industry, either through film or literary work was Helena Blavatsky.

Helena Petrovna Hahn (1831-1891), better known as Madame Blavatsky, was the founder of Theosophy as it regards to occult ideology and influence.

She was born in Ekaterinoslav (now Dnepropetrovsk), Ukraine, the daughter of Col. Peter Alexeivich von Hahn and Elena Fadeev. Her mother, also known as Helena Andreyvna Fadeyev, was a novelist.

She married, on July 7, 1849, Nikifor Vassilievitch Blavatsky. He died several years later and she soon married her second husband, Michael C. Betanelly on April 3, 1875. She maintained that neither marriage was consummated. She separated from Betanelly after a few months.

Madame Blavatsky traveled throughout the world, and resided in New York City from 1873 to 1878.

She then founded, with Henry Steel Olcott, William Quan Judge and others, the Theosophical Society (T.S.), a new religious movement of the late nineteenth century that took its inspiration from Hinduism and Buddhism. Blavatsky claimed to have been given access to what she called a 'secret doctrine' that had been passed down the ages from ancient sages of a White Brotherhood. In this respect Blavatsky's ideas followed in the tradition of Freemasonry and Rosicrucianism.

The difference was that Blavatsky's esoteric wisdom was supposed to be derived from Eastern sages, rather than from European esoteric currents. In particular, she pointed to the Mahatmas ("great souls") Morya and Koot Hoomi as her particular guides in the establishment of the T.S. In recent years, the scholarship of K. Paul Johnson has made important inroads on the historical identities of Blavatsky's "Masters," considering them as living human individuals (supernaturally empowered or not) of their period, rather than unearthly super beings or legitimizing fabrications.

Furthermore, Blavatsky claimed that the ancient "Akashic" wisdom to which she had access was consistent with modern science, in particular with physics and evolutionary biology (for instance borrowing the name Lemuria from biologist P.L. Sclater as the name for the origin of her lost continent which would serve as the origin for her third root race). This claim that esoteric spiritual knowledge is consistent with new science may be considered to be the first instance of what is now called New Age thinking. In fact, many researchers feel that much of New Age-thought started with Blavatsky.

Aleister Crowley recognized Blavatsky as a Sister of A.'.A.'. (i.e. a Master of the Temple 8°=3# in his system of spiritual grades), specifically pointing her out as his immediate predecessor in "The Temple of Truth," published in The Heart of the Master through O.T.O. in 1938. He thought it especially noteworthy that he was born in the same year that the Theosophical Society was inaugurated. Crowley reissued Blavatsky's Voice of the Silence (Extracts from the Book of the Golden Precepts, including "The Two Paths" and "The Seven Portals") with his own commentary as Liber LXXI, a Class B publication of A.'.A.'.

Blavatsky died in London, England.

Aleister Crowley

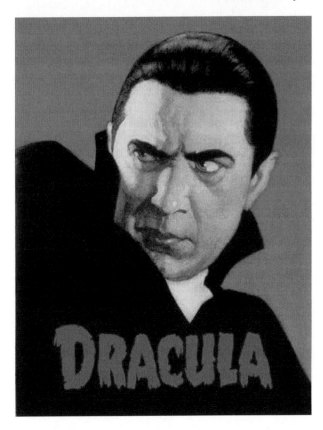

Vincent Price

Peter Cushing

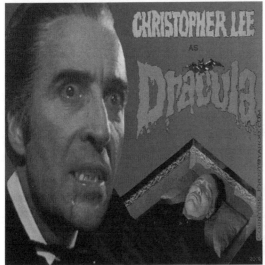

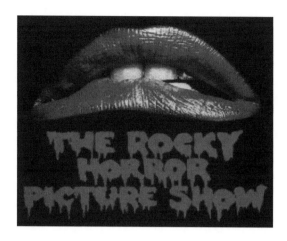

Bela Lugosi, a Hungarian born actor, famous for his portrayal of Count Dracula in Todd Browning's film depiction of Bram Stoker's novel, was a student of the occult himself. Often depressed, Lugosi would comment to others of his never ending nightmares where he would see visions of his own death. At times Lugosi would state that he felt something greater than he coming against him; he would often wake from his sleep exhausted from the night events which plagued him. No doubt his work within the field of his character caused much of his oppression. Let it never be forgotten that we are spiritual beings, subject to either Godly influence or Satanic influence. I have no doubt Lugosi was being subjected to demonic forces all because of his own personal involvement in the portrayal of a demonic character called Dracula.

Horror films, like other subjects which deal with the occult, come from sources which use fear and disbelief in its creation. Every aspect of a horror movie, from its initial creation, its script development and ultimately its arrival onto the screen, uses it's roots based in the occult, paganism and idolatry to gain a following as well as influence those who watch them. The power of suggestion within each frame is inspired by one key component - spiritual seduction.

Not only do horror films have a foundation in the occult, they also can be a powerful as well as influential tool in the teaching of Satanism, witchcraft and black magic. Horror films have the basic built in requirements for the seeker of mysticism to learn and study the craft. Films like the Omen series, Beyond the Door (1977), Satan's School for Girls (1973), Born of Fire (1983), and others often portray a connection almost religiously to Satan. Walt Disney's Fantasia (1940) which has a stunning depiction of the Russian devil Chernabog for Mussorgsky's Night on Bald Mountain symphonic poem – itself a Satanic inspiration.

The horror film, The Devils Rain (1975) was the first to actually bring onto the production a Satanist, but not just any Satanist, but THE Satanist - Anton LaVey. Anton LaVey was the founder of the Church of Satan, a San Francisco based cult established in 1966 by LaVey and a small group of followers. As technical consultant to The Devil's Rain, like Aleister Crowley before him, Anton LaVey equally began to fulfill a role to many Hollywood producer, director and actor who ventured into the dark world of horror films.

Yet no other film in the horror genre to date can accurately portray Satanism, encourage it as well as celebrate it the way the 1968 cult film, "Rosemary's Baby" did. One year after the release of Rosemary's Baby, Director Roman Polanski suffered a horrible event in his own life, the death of his wife, Sharon Tate, who also was pregnant with their first child by the followers of Charles Manson. It should be noted that Susan Atkins, the member of the Manson family who later murdered Polanski's pregnant wife Sharon Tate, was an ex-follower of Anton LaVey. Anton LaVey, it is believed, played the unaccredited role of Satan during the impregnation scene.

Many however see the movie as an occult manifesto, heralding a new era. Rosemary's Baby is Aleister Crowley's "Child of the new Aeon", or Horus the son of Isis – the bringer of a new era in world history. Whether it was intentional or not, Rosemary's Baby did appear at the brink of a new era and became part of an important social change. It was Anton LaVey himself who praised the film as an accurate portrayal of a secret religious cult now being thrust into the lime light. If there was ever a film which would establish the union of occult and entertainment, it was indeed Rosemary's Baby. The roots of Satanism and horror films had now been baptized in the river of idolatry and anointed to bring about a wake of lies, deceit and idolatry in it's path.

Yet the circle was not complete. The connections between Polanski's Rosemary's Baby and Anton LaVey or Aleister Crowley didn't end with these men or even Susan Atkins, but others apart of the horror film inner circle of followers and creators went deeper, much deeper.

Kenneth Anger, horror film director, made his first important film, Fireworks, in 1947, completing it in two weekends. It was a highly personalized psychodrama featuring himself playing a guilt-filled gay man dreaming of being beaten by a group of sailors which leads him to sexual freedom. In 1949, the highly acclaimed film was shown to the public at Jean Cocteau's "Festival of the Damned" in Biarritz. Much of Anger's work was completed in France and other European countries. Many of his works, such as The Story of O, remain uncompleted.

Anger was not only a student of Aleister Crowley, but he was member and practicer of the occult, who later, with his inner relationship with Anton LaVey, would go on to become a member of the Church of Satan. In 1967 Anger had directed a film called Lucifer Rising, starring Manson follower Bobby Beausoleil. Another follower and Tate-killer, Susan Atkins, had appeared with LaVey in performances at a Los Angeles area strip club. To this day, Kenneth Anger reacts with a sense of fondness when he recalls his time in the company of such men like Crowley and LaVey. The circle was growing.

Can we state that Rosemary's Baby caused the death of Sharon Tate or victimize many of those who have suffered under the film and those who connected with it? Yes and no. The word tells us that the penalty for sin is death (Romans 6:23). Whenever we venture into Satan's domain, when we purposely allow ourselves to be involved in things which God strictly forbids, then we willingly open ourselves up to demonic influence and in many cases, we allow Satan the legal, spiritual right to have his way over our lives. But worse, if we do not have a relationship with Jesus Christ, if we have not submitted ourselves to him, repented of our sins and confess him as Lord and Savior, then we are lost, we are in fact children of the Devil, meaning, there is no relationship nor is there protection from destruction. This is the reason many have fallen into terrible events, accidents, tormented at night by dreams, even demonic oppression and at times, possession, because God has no right to their life and thus, Satan takes ownership and many times, he succeeds in his original plan, to kill, steal and destroy.

Horror films clearly have occult roots; they are submersed in lies and deceit and devoid of anything of purpose other than to manipulate and subject the viewer to a spiritual world of darkness, demonic control and ultimately bring about a worship of things unholy. The horror film is an enemy of the cross, for it projects everything Christ resented, it's roots in Satanism, black magic, sorcery, witchcraft, necromancy, they are all traits of a delusion, a celebration of evil.

The history, the link to horror films not only brings a person into bondage, but they give Satan the praise and worship he desires. Satan desires praise, he demands worship and he uses horror films as a medium to be worshiped and praised. Is it any great wonder that every major horror movie that has ever been created uses one of the above mentioned tools of the occult? From devil worship to human sacrifice, from rape in the form of necrophilia, to immoral sex acts, these ingredients combined with Satanism and witchcraft bring about a level of glorification to Satan and his kingdom. It is these reasons alone that we need to take into account just what his kingdom truly is about, and why we must avoid all appearance of evil. Horror movies are rooted in evil, they are destructive and dangerous and those who partake of them are not wise.

Chapter Three
Bram Stoker

Abraham Bram Stoker was born November 8th, 1847 in Dublin Ireland. Novelist and short story writer, Bram Stoker received modest success early in his career until 1897, it was during that period when Stoker published what would go on to become the most popular horror novel to date - Dracula.

Stoker was bed-ridden until he started school at the age of seven, when he made a complete recovery. Of this time, Stoker wrote, "I was naturally thoughtful, and the leisure of long illness gave opportunity for many thoughts which were fruitful according to their kind in later years." He was educated in a private school run by the Rev. William Woods.

After his recovery, he grew up without further major health issues, even excelling as an athlete (he was named University Athlete) at Trinity College, Dublin, which he attended from 1864 to 1870. He graduated with honors in mathematics. He was auditor of the College Historical Society and president of the University Philosophical Society, where his first paper was on "Sensationalism in Fiction and Society".

Stoker was educated at Trinity College, "where he won honors in science, mathematics, oratory, history, and composition ("Obituary"). After graduating he entered the Irish Civil Service where he served as Inspector of Petty Sessions. In 1876 Stoker met the actor Henry Irving and by 1878 had moved to London where he was acting manager at the famous Lyceum Theatre. It was there that Stoker entered into fashionable circles through which we learn much of his character and influences. In the same year Stoker married Florence Balcombe, who was also courted by Oscar Wilde. There has been much speculation about the Stokers' family dynamic, some of which suggests that the marriage was loveless. The Stokers' only child, Noel, was born in 1879.

Stoker's interest in the supernatural and the occult — which would become a salient focus for his later fiction — may have been rooted in his unidentified childhood illness, which supposedly kept him bed-ridden until the age of seven; this seclusion would be compounded by an interest in Irish folklore, which often concerned tales of bogeys and vampires. In fact, Stoker's later interests included "Egyptology, Babylonian lore, astral projections, and alchemy"

Throughout much of his career, Stoker interest in the occult deepened with insights into witchcraft as well as Satanism. Stoker had become so interested in the occult that he joined the secret occult society, Hermetic Order of the Golden Dawn. A coven of occult believers whose members included none other than Aleister Crowley.

To better understand just how connected these men (and women) were with the occult and more importantly the Satanic rites within their coven (Order of the Golden Dawn), it's important to understand just who was apart of this inner, private circle of literary prowess. Members included such notables such as William Butler Yeats, Maud Gonne, Constance Wilde, (the wife of Oscar

Wilde), Arthur Machen, Moina Bergson, Arthur Edward Waite, Florence Farr and Algernon Blackwood.

The Golden Dawn's contribution to the Western Magical Tradition is definitely worth noting, because it was their synthesis of the Kabbalah, alchemy, tarot, astrology, divination, numerology, Masonic symbolism, and ritual magic into one coherent and logical system which led them to influence countless occult organizations to come. These associations clearly helped in some part, to bring about Bram's eventual work in Dracula and started a movement which has remained nearly 200 years later.

What influenced Stoker to create his vampire novel? What inspiration could have inspired him to create one of the most dark characters of literature? The answer, I believe, can be traced to the word of God. Romans 1:29-30 says, "Being filled with all unrighteousness, fornication, wickedness, covetousness, maliciousness; full of envy, murder, debate, deceit, malignity; whisperers, backbiters, hateful to God, insolent, haughty, boastful, <u>inventors of evil things,</u> disobedient to parents."

There is no question that the Apostle Paul was clearly speaking about the world and those who lived in it in the last days. Even though the time frame of Bram's work would be in the late 1890's, the proof of Satanic influence and his work to endure this long suggests a more sinister mastermind is at work here. Yes, there are works of literary fame which have long endured the pages of time and influence many, but none to date has had the remarkable endurance and longevity as Dracula has. Only a few fictional works can boast of outlasting one generation to the next and still be relevant.

To put it mildly, Dracula is evil, it's central character, an undead count, is the representation of evil. Even the actual meaning of his name - Dracula, literally means "Son of the Devil". While it is true that Stoker, throughout his travels in eastern Europe, became familiar with the story of Vlad Dracula, otherwise known as Vlad the impaler, the accounts of Stoker's work and how he drew from another source to create such a vivid character as a modern day vampire which has lived for centuries, says something more of Stoker's past association with Aleister Crowley and the secret order he belonged to. More importantly, it speaks to the spirit of influence that the occult and the Satanic order Stoker belonged to which had more affect on his creation rather than influence by historical figures.

When one reads "Dracula", one can get the full aspect of how Bram Stoker felt about Christianity. Coming from a strict, Christian family himself, Stoker seems to equate anti-Christ qualities in the framework of his character of Dracula, a rebellious Lord who poured out his own sense of moral judgment upon those within his kingdom as well as those who would come against his reign. Stoker clearly was hostile to the thought which said there is but one God, one pathway to salvation, through Jesus Christ. Yet Stoker seems to push his resentment and hatred of all that is good and holy in the realm of Christ by subjecting those traits and personalities of individuals in the pages of his classic literary piece as foolish, superstitious fools. How ironic that Bram would pen such words as his own disdain toward Christian beliefs by calling them superstitious, yet he himself placed so much energy, time and belief in the very religions of this world, such as his membership to the Golden Dawn.

Bram Stoker remained defiant throughout his life toward Christianity and God and by all accounts, left this world in the same state as he lived it, in rebellion. Yet, even with all the success he has earned throughout the centuries for his literary work, he still remains subjected to the true reality and that was, unless a man has been born again, repented of his sins, he shall not enter into the kingdom of Heaven. Equally sadder still, Bram Stoker was victim to a greater abuse, where he himself can only now realize in the eternal doom which awaited him as he passed from this life to the next, in that he was merely a pawn by Satan.

Chapter Four
Seduction of Evil

In November 2008, one of the most anticipated films since Harry Potter debuted to movie audiences across the country and a cult following was born. Grossing 35.7 million on its opening day, Twilight became the latest in Hollywood's offering of vampirism. Horror fans soon began to appreciate the modern day vampire and within months, impressionable young teen girls began to fall in love with Edward, the films main vampire character. What followed was anything film producers could ever imagine, for not since the Harry Potter franchise, which captured the hearts of children around the world, yet was beginning to see its popularity fade, a new birth of cult followers were lining up to see this modern day vampire version of Romeo and Juliet.

With the success of 2008's Twilight, the film went on to generate three (3) additional films, Twilight Saga (New Moon), Twilight Saga (Eclipse), and Twilight Saga (Breaking Dawn). Grossing 2 billion in total revenue, Twilight has gone on to become the 4th largest movie trilogy in overall domestic and foreign sales.

The allurement of evil is a powerful one. Satan is extremely clever when he paints a seductive picture to entice and seduce potential victims, and one of the ways he does so is by using our basic appeal of emotion. Anger, sadness, hate, they are emotional components of our very existence as human beings, but one other aspect of emotion which Satan uses most is the very aspect which every human feels and desires, either in giving or receiving, which is LOVE.

The popularity of Stephenie Meyer's Twilight series represents the changing times of not just films, but culture as well. Movies in the past, from such films as Gone With the Wind, Terms of Endearment, Schindlers List and The Way We Were, although popular with audiences, never struck a chord with their generation as Twilight or even Harry Potter has had on the current generation. It seems that this particular generation unlike past decades, is a generation which not only embraces the occult, but it longs for something to believe in. What Twilight did for many young people, especially women, is give a false sense of hope through a main character (Edward) which suggests that something evil can satisfy the heart and soul of a person, even if only a fictional character, it has done more harm than good.

Consider the way Edward is written:

1. He is able to read minds.
2. He has superhuman strength.
3. He has superhuman speed.
4. He consistently exhibits strong self-control.
5. He is loving, kind, and thoughtful.
6. He is self-sacrificing.
7. He is tender and sensitive.
8. He is lavishly generous.

9. He anticipates Bella's needs and desires.
10. He sparkles in the sunlight with a stunning radiance.

To young impressionable girls, Edward appeals to their deepest desires of feeling wanted, protected, sheltered and most importantly - loved. The love many women feel over Edward is more, dare I say, lustful, rather than a physical an emotional love. This aspect of Edward - a vampire, projects the idea of "forbidden fruit". Women want him and men want to be him. It's a greater symptom of the spiritual and moral quandary we find ourselves in as this culture begins to adapt to things which God specifically hates which are morally and spiritually wrong.

It must be noted that vampirism is a direct representation of Satanism. From the circle where Satanist's as well as Wicca's use as a medium of power, to the selection of followers (vampires equally select their members the same way); the central core to both Satanist's and Vampires is the blood. Satanist's initiates their members into the coven thru a blood ritual while Vampires use the transference of blood from the victim to the vampire thus making the victim a member into the vampire coven.

Movies such as Twilight, Halloween, Friday the 13th and Saw, shows a more deeper fascination to the occult and reflect somewhat of a spiritual desire about the unknown, to be more accurate, the darkness of evil. The allure of horror films among teens and young adults indicate the stronghold of dark forces which seem to resonate with many movie fans because it (horror films) satisfy certain appeal about the afterlife. There is something about being frightened, scared or terrorized by something unknown which appeals to the central core of us as human beings, but should we allow ourselves to be placed in a state of such fear? The answer is no!

In God's perfect kingdom there is no darkness, equally, there is no fear, no worry, nothing to be frightened by, nor is there a boogeyman to worry about. There is only peace, joy and contentment. When God created the earth, it was perfect, void of evil and chaos, the darkness, which was night, was not something to be feared, but to be embraced, "God saw all that he had made, and it was very good. And there was evening, and there was morning--the sixth day." Genesis 1:31. But because of sin, rebellion by one man - Adam, as well as the fall of Lucifer, the world fell into darkness. From that point, darkness began to take on another aspect, and that aspect was to hide evil.

There has always been the fascination of the occult and the supernatural; it goes back to our basic instincts of desiring to know what lies ahead once this life is over. Man has always sought to understand or even grasp death. Is there an eternity? Is there life after death? Is there a heaven or hell? Is there a God? It's our natural, inner being that seeks these questions out, and the truth is, this is actually how God intended it to be. God gave each of us intellect and that intellect serves an original purpose, and that original purpose was and still is, to seek God, or to be more specific - Jesus Christ.

The problem with our basic instinct to seek God and his righteousness is that Satan equally understands and knows our basic condition as well, his whole purpose is to "steal, kill and destroy", and he uses deception thru false religion, science, the human intellect to steer men away from Christ. Satan doesn't want men to know the truth, but he wants men to believe a lie and be damned for all eternity. Satan knows his end is the lake of fire and eternal destruction, so in his angelic mind, he creates things to deceive humanity to drag their souls down with him. This is where the occult comes into play.

As I stated before, man seeks to understand the unknown and so Satan gives man a singular idea and that idea is, he (man) doesn't need God or his son, but he can reach the "other" world through methods and rituals built on demonic influence and teachings. Anything Satan can do to deceive mankind, he will use for his ultimate benefit to destroy humanity. This is why, thousands of years ago, Satan, through fallen angels, came down to men and dwelt among them, taught them mythology, satanic ideas, occult practices and man believed and accepted it, hook, line and sinker. From that point in time and throughout the ages until our present time, the depths of demonic influence grew, religion and occult practices from Egyptian worship, the Druids of Europe and the witches of Salem, man's involvement and desire for forbidden subjects grew and has carried over into a new form of media, not etched in stone or parchment paper, but through the use of celluloid.

No other form of communication of the past can boast the same powerful influence upon a culture the way motion pictures has had on this particular society. Movies can be a powerful medium when it comes to stirring up the human spirit such as, evoke an emotion, induce fear, arouse sexually, conjure up anger or trigger sadness. Films have that ability. It's that same ability that, under demonic influence, causes many to involve themselves with subjects such as the occult, which actually indoctrinates the viewer to ideas which promote evil and idolatry.

When John Carpenter released his 1978 classic, "Halloween", the film did more than just grab movie audiences; it was, in my opinion, a turning point for horror films to begin incorporating themes relating to the occult and witchcraft. Carpenter, an avid atheist himself, created a film as well as a character which depicted not just serial violence, but supernatural violence. The character "Michael Meyers" was the first horror film character created symbolizing relentless evil, stalking its prey in an attempt to murder its victims in the most horrific manner.

It was this depiction of "Michael Meyers", set against the backdrop of Halloween which represented the ancient pagan holiday of the Druids, was the first horror film of the 20th century to marry the occult and suspense as one unified form of evil, and movie audiences loved it. The success of "Halloween" proved that society was drastically changing, accepting imagery of violence and horror as a normal aspect of its generation. What would follow would be a flood gate of horror films which not only depicted raw violence, but the embrace of subjects such as necromancy, witchcraft, black magic, human sacrifice and necrophilia. Halloween, I believe, was the avenue in which Satan was waiting for, the tool he used through influence of one particular director, namely John Carpenter, to release upon a culture demonic influences that has, to this day, done more to open more people to the occult and the supernatural than anything Aleister Crowley or Anton LaVey could ever have done.

What is the appeal of horror films? Why do people love being scared? What is this dark appeal of people wanting to allow themselves to be influenced and entertained by something designed to terrify them? The answer can be found in Genesis 6:5, "And God saw that the wickedness of man was great in the earth, and that every imagination of the thoughts of his heart was only evil continually."

There is an aspect of a heart not desiring God's word or, in this case, desiring things which are evil, such as the modern horror film that signals someone not desiring holiness or righteousness. People who desire and love horror films, with its depictions of murder, sexual imagery such as nudity and sex, depictions of the occult, such as human sacrifice and the conjuring of demonic spirits, speaks greatly to the spiritual aspect of that person who desires something like the modern horror film.

The appeal of films such as Friday the 13th, Hellraiser, or Poltergeist has much to do with playing with subject matter which is strictly forbidden, yet desired by most. Why? I believe it's because people, when given the opportunity to delve into areas which are spiritually harmful, they feel as though they are getting certain insight into the unknown whether they are conscious of it or not. The inner craving for spiritual enlightenment, combined with the desire for false spirituality and a basic need for sexual stimulation, produces the right formula for someone to be deceived by a Satanic lie.

As long as people continue to desire things which God prohibits, as long as people reject God's truth found in his word, the more they will be given over to strongholds which not only hinder one's growth, but influence them in ways which leads to oppression and often times spiritual bondage. In almost every case study where men who were convicted of either rape or even worse, murder, there was one component in their pattern of influence which they all eventually acknowledged and that was horror films. Horror films are not only mere entertainment, but they can lead people into areas of real life bondage like no other. This is not God's way; actually, those who are in Christ are commanded NOT to involve themselves in the occult, or images which promote wickedness or perversion. Horror films, regardless of what many would say are neither hurtful or harmful, is a lie in of itself, for there are signals within horror movies which reflect a deeper core truth and that truth is that God is absent from man and that man is on his own, subject to the will of the universe, or fate. This is all another lie, another scheme by many who would push the agenda of horror movies upon an unsuspecting world.

Chapter Five
Sex and Nudity in Horror

It's almost impossible these days to watch a standard horror film and not see nudity or even sexual acts between people, equally hard is not to see some form of sexual suggestion in most PG-13 horror films. The question which we need to ask is why? Why are horror films and sex like two components which are virtually inseparable? Is there formula for this? The answer is yes, it is in fact a formula which goes back to the basic foundation of horror films and pagan worship.

Nudity used in horror movies is often times a symbolization of innocence. When nudity is used in this way in a horror movie or story, it is to point out that the character is innocent, and without the tight bindings of sin.

In most cases, nudity in horror movies is meant to point out characters that have, "sinned," in some way (usually having underage sex) and is in line to be killed by the antagonist of the movie. You will notice that many of the characters that die in horror movies that have nude scenes, either die while they are naked, or just after becoming clothed.

The symbolism is equal to the rituals found in many pagans, Wicca and, in some cases, Satanic circles. In almost every aspect of occult rituals, sex and nudity can almost always be found. In his 1969 "Bible" - the Satanic Bible, Anton LaVey states the following in regards to sex and nudity in the coven, "If all parties involved are mature adults who willingly take full responsibility for their actions and voluntarily engage in a given form of sexual expression - even if it is generally considered taboo - then there is no reason for them to suppress their sexual inclination."

In almost every aspect of ancient pagan practices, nudity, (as well as sex) literally goes hand in hand. The pagan religion Hieros Gamos, or Sacred marriage ritual is one aspect of this type of ritual which is still observed today. Records of this ceremony have been dated as far back as early Sumerian, about 5500 years ago. In this ritual the high priestess acting as avatar of The Goddess, had sex with the ruler of the country to show the Goddess's acceptance of him as ruler and caretaker of her people. The use of sex and nudity was the great act of submission for those involved in this ancient, pagan practice.

This aspect of the use of sex and nudity can be found in almost every function of the early pagan customs, but equally, they are found in other areas as well, namely anything which deals with the occult as we have established. So why horror films?

As we have previously discussed in the first chapter dealing with the foundational aspects of horror and its direct connection to the occult, it goes to reason that the significance of nudity in horror films is a ritual in of itself. After all, if horror films are the perfect medium and tool to indoctrinate and influence people by way of glorifying occultist practices, then it can be equally assumed that when sex and/or nudity are used within the framework of a horror movie, it is establishing the direct link back to that original foundation - Satanic influence.

When a person watches a young woman remove her clothes to become naked, then becomes sexually active on screen within a horror movie, she, as well as the young man (if applicable) are now partaking of a Satanic ritual within the movie itself and the viewer, or audience, are none the wiser.

Nudity, in particular with horror films, reflects witchcraft and it's called Skyclad. That term is considered to be a "natural" ritual form of participation by Witches, which during their worship times nothing will come between their "energy" and the "energy" they might receive in their worship rituals; for Satanism, it is to be the polar opposite of Biblical Principles (black for white), the same goes for sexual practices. Many have multiple reasons why they do what they do because of the whims or likes/dislikes of the coven leaders for either practice (nudity or sexual activity). Ego driven worship styles follows each leader so no true rules of engagement exist just the generalities afore mentioned.

When we see nudity within the context of a horror film, what we are seeing is directly related to the occult ritual found in Witchcraft. Every horror film that depicts nudity or even sexual acts, do so under the guise of paying tribute to this ancient craft, whether or not the creators designed it that way or not, nudity is part of the overall aspect of Satan worship and horror films, thru the means of nudity, pays homage to that fact.

In the other, more obvious reason why we see so much nudity in films, especially in the horror genre, besides the obvious occult reference is money, sex sells.

Chapter Six
The British are coming!

When America was being swamped by Universal Pictures and RKO during the 1930's through the 1950's with its own version of horror, another form of horror/suspense was beginning to rise in another part of the world, the very place where much of horror got its very foundation - England.

By the end of the 1950's, America had come out of a world war, a hard recession and things were now greatly improving, especially in the world of media, for another form of entertainment was beginning to grow, one that would eventually change how the American people received their information, such as news, weather and sports. Even the method of traditional means of watching entertainment - the theater, was being pushed aside to make way for a brand new medium - television.

While America was glowing in its second birth, across the vast Atlantic ocean, in the heart of Britain, another aspect of horror films was taking shape and one which would literally impact the way others looked at horror films; it was the foundation of old principles combined with the new ideology creeping across the world.

William Hinds was born in 1887, by the time he was in his 50's, Hinds and his business partner - Enrique Carreras, set out to form Hammer Films Ltd. It was through this venture that would birth a new breed of occult horror films based on works by writers and authors who, by their own right, were connected in one way or the other, with occultist sects or secret orders. For it was in 1957 that Hinds, an avid cyclist, met his death while riding near his Leatherhead home. It was through this event which would allow Hind's second son, Anthony Hinds, to literally take the reigns of his Father's company, along with Carreras's son - James, and re-build Hammer into a solid film company whose foundation was pure horror.

For several years, beginning in the mid 1960's, Hammer began to tackle subjects of ancient religions, mainly pagan and Satan worship. Their close relationship with Dennis Wheatley proved to be a successful one, as Wheatley, a close personal friend of Aleister Crowley as well as a member of a secret, occultist order himself, seemed a perfect pair. It was almost as if their relationship (Hammer and Wheatley) was a match made for each other.

Witchcraft was one of Wheatley's favorite subjects and it was that influence which helped him pen the novel, "The Devil Rides Out", which Hammer Studios was only to willing to push for a feature film version of Wheatley's successful book. He was an acknowledged master of stories about black magic like no other for his time. It was his personal experience about black magic and occult ceremonies that seemed to leap off the pages of "The Devil Rides Out" and influenced Hammer enough to draw not only the Studio's involvement into making it's first film about the occult, but it was also British born actor Christopher Lee's personal involvement himself which drew Hammer into making The Devil Rides Out.

Lee, an practicing occultist himself, convinced the Studio that Wheatley's novel deserved it's moment on the silver screen. Yet, it was Wheatley's convincing portrayal of authentic devil worship that made the film a hit with many fans of horror.

Wheatley's first occult ceremony, took place in Wales, at Trelyden Hall near Welshpool, the home of long-standing friends of the Wheatleys, Charles and Joan Beatty, or Joan Grant as she is better known. It was a pleasant, rambling old house where Charles Beatty practiced magic rituals and strange rites which included what he called a Ceremony of the Roses, one magical ceremony that Joan and Dennis Wheatley did witness.

The rose is, of course, a very ancient magical symbol, and those curious practitioners of the occult arts known as the Brethren of the Rosy Cross, or Rosicrucians, took for their badge or chief symbol a rose – and combined it with a cross. The rose was the symbol of Venus, the goddess of erotic love, and legend has it that the origin of the rose can be found in the blood of Venus, when wounded by Cupid's dart. The rose was also the symbol of secrecy.

Dennis related to a friend that what interested him most during the Ceremony of the Roses as practiced by Joan and Charles Beatty, apart from the obviously erotic element, was the element of power that pervaded Charles during his performance of the ceremony. Dennis already knew Aleister Crowley and he thought that Crowley had really succeeded on at least one occasion in raising Pan; he stated privately to a friend about one incident that had convinced him that Crowley possessed or could conjure up occult power.

While still an undergraduate at Cambridge, Crowley was already deeply interested in the occult sciences, and he was very keen to get the university dramatic society to put on a play by Aristophanes, during the course of which he intended to perform some authentic spells. When the Master of John's College refused to allow any such thing, Crowley was annoyed. He manufactured a wax figure of the Master and, with a coven he had formed among his friends at the university, he created the atmosphere, chanted a spell and was preparing to thrust a large needle into the image when one of his friends lost his nerve, broke the circle and grabbed Crowley's arm. The deflected needle pierced the ankle of the image, and the circle broke up in disarray. Next day the Master did not appear and he was incapacitated for weeks with a broken ankle. Whatever the explanation of that particular incident, which Dennis had heard from several different sources – and it was put about that the Master had fallen down some steps – Dennis sensed in Crowley a sensuous and hidden power that he now recognized in Charles Beatty. Whether it was because of the mumbo-jumbo associated with him or in spite of it, it made a deep impression on Dennis and he believed some people did possess a hidden power that could be used for good or for evil purposes.

That Ceremony of the Roses that he and Joan witnessed was held in a darkened room, with light concentrated on a sofa covered with black velvet and sprinkled with rose petals. Joan Beatty entered wearing a long cloak fastened at the neck with a silver clasp in the shape of a rose. Charles, also wearing a long dark cloak proceeded to address Joan and shower her with rose petals from a huge bowl on a table at the side of the sofa; after making various passes with a sword and speaking quietly to her, he seemed to put her into some kind of trance.

In the otherwise dead silence Charles continued quietly to issue commands to her and she appeared to writhe and breathe deeply as he continued his abjurations and then, after a few more passes with his sword and sprinkling with rose petals, she raised one hand as though in a dream and unclasped her cloak; when it dropped to the floor, it revealed that she was completely naked. She raised her hands above her head, looked upwards as directed by her husband and, as she stood there, like a statue, Charles flicked more rosewater and rose petals all over her body, which was denuded of all body hair. When her body was glistening and quivering in ecstasy, he led her to the sofa, where she lay in an abandoned position. He anointed her whole body with some aromatic oil until she appeared to be in an ecstatic condition, writhing and contorting her body sensually in tune with the administration of his hands. The tension mounted as she stretched and raised herself to meet his hands as they stroked and darted all over her body; soon his lips replaced his hands and eventually Joan reached and passed a fever pitch of excitement. As she became calmer and lay as though asleep but with her eyes open, Charles ceased to touch her and after making a number of passes over her inert body, in a low, monotonous voice he commanded her to speak – or could it all have been in Dennis's vivid imagination?

She talked, Dennis related, as though she was in a previous incarnation, in ancient Egypt in fact, and the Wheatleys listened fascinated as Charles took down every word she uttered. He seemed obsessed with traditional occult symbolism and ceremonies, and it seemed to Dennis that his concentration and power influenced whatever powers were abroad that night. Joan Beatty spoke in every way as though she was living in Egypt centuries ago, and the Wheatleys never forgot that strange and striking ceremony. Dennis in particular was certain that some kind of power that was not of this world flowed between Charles and his wife that night, and he not only used some of the rituals and ideas that he witnessed that night in future books but also became very aware that reincarnation could well be a fact.

What came out of this was The Devil Rides Out, with Hammer, along with actor Christopher Lee, made their movie, all based on the actual events of devil worship. Hammer Studios went on to become a popular film studio creating erotic, Shakespearean horror films, but it's claim to fame was none other than its own version of Bram Stoker's Dracula, starring occultist actor Christopher Lee.

 More than anything else, the Hammer Studios wanted to attract a significant portion of the adult market to the horror film genre. Instead of banal scripts and terrible acting, the Universal story lines would be updated for that targeted audience with experienced actors like Christopher Lee (Count Dracula) and Peter Cushing (Dr. Victor Frankenstein) at the helm, delivering lines with vigor and enthusiasm. Perhaps the most salient addition was the effective use of bloodshed and gore at key moments to illustrate just how despicable these characters were to their unsuspecting victims. The movies were shot in a Technicolor brilliance (unlike their monochromatic predecessors), which only exaggerated the death scenes. Now the viewer would gaze at streams of blood gushing out from chests, necks, and faces in a potpourri of deep reds and bright purples amidst softer blue and green backdrops. Some examples of Hammer Studios' seventeen-year tenure in the horror cinema (from 1957 to 1974) are included to show just how much the Destroyer archetype had been modified to satiate the public demand for more atypical and bizarre ways of killing on the screen.

The Dracula series of films began their run with some very striking scenes. In Horror of Dracula (1958) Van Helsing drives the stake into a recently converted vampire with a sickening relish. By the ending he traps Dracula in his own castle and, holding candlesticks in the sign of the cross, the good doctor forces the Count directly into the rays of the sun, thereby blasting the crumbling body to dusty remains. The follow-up movie, Dracula—Prince of Darkness (1965), involves the resurrection of the infamous monster by having his manservant brutally slit the throat of one of the guests at the castle in a Black Mass ritual. Dracula Has Risen from the Grave (1969) depicts one of the most graphic sequences of any vampire film to date. Here the Count survives a staking by pulling out the pointed object and throwing it at his attackers, but not before a significant amount of blackish red blood comes streaming out of the rather large hole made in the vampire's chest. As the titles progressed, Dracula would be stabbed, burnt, poked and prodded atop a bed of stakes, and even shoveled to death (Dracula A.D., 1972) before meeting his screen finale at the hands of Van Helsing once more in The Satanic Rites of Dracula (1973).

Like Dracula, the Frankenstein set had its share of memorable death moments. Beginning with The Curse of Frankenstein (1957), the Monster strangles a number of the local villagers with its bare hands before being shot directly in the face. The film critic John McCarty notes that Frankenstein is no better than his creation, "fondling brains, eyeballs, severed hands and other assorted organs" throughout the film with an unusual coldness that would bring new meaning to the term "mad scientist" (McCarty 1990, p. 19).

The series continues this bloody path by having new creations eat the flesh of their victims (Revenge of Frankenstein, 1959) as well as decapitate assorted bullies and store their heads in picnic baskets and atop bedposts (Frankenstein Created Woman, 1967). Perhaps the most tragic of all fates occurs for the Monster when it is literally torn apart by the inmates of an asylum who spurn it for being so different from themselves (Frankenstein and the Monster from Hell, 1974).

In addition to the Dracula and Frankenstein films, Hammer Studios also produced one Wolf man picture. The Curse of the Werewolf (1961) ends on a sad note when the cursed creature's father shoots it in the heart with a silver bullet. The metamorphosis back to the human state never transpires, and so the camera lingers on the were-wolf's face that has bloodstained tears dripping from the permanently open, yet forlorn, eyes.

Other British companies tried to emulate the Hammer horror treatments with some measure of success. The Amicus Company specialized in reanimated body parts that would seek out with a vengeance those parties responsible for their owners' deaths (see Dr. Terror's House of Horrors, 1965; Tales from the Crypt, 1972; Asylum, 1972; And Now the Screaming Starts, 1973).

Elstree Studios, in conjunction with American International, gave a more human face to the Destroyer by casting horror film veteran Vincent Price in the title role of The Abominable Dr. Phibes (1971), who metes out justice to those physicians who could not save his beloved wife, Victoria.

In 1992 Price disclosed in an interview with Stanley Wiater that he thoroughly enjoyed making Dr. Phibes, as it enabled him to throw a good deal of humor into the role so that the extent of his violent acts could be significantly diminished on the screen. And so one of Phibes's victims is drained entirely of his blood, another has the flesh on her face consumed by locusts, and still another is eaten alive in the cockpit of his plane by ravenous rats while the doctor attentively listens to his assistant Vulnavia playing beautiful music upon her violin. The send-up formula would be employed at least three more times by Price (in Dr. Phibes Rises Again, 1972; Theater of Blood, 1973; and Madhouse, 1974) until the actor became tired of the same old story line and eventually retired from the horror genre. But the violence and humor combination would remain a staple of the horror film from this point on.

Hammer's "Dracula" went on to great success with movie fans, yet, it's continuance to portray occult symbolism, its celebration of Satanic influence and its boldness in flaunting erotica by portraying women in sexual imagery, made Hammer a promoter of films which did nothing more than give Satan the glory and praise he has earnestly sought and has brought millions of young people under the spell of occult and sexual bondage.

Another British studio which began to grow amongst the success of Hammer was Amicus Studios. Between the 1950s and early 70s the first name in British horror and fantasy film making was Hammer, whose Gothic horror movies inspired a generation of film makers across the world, and whose ventures into everything from science fiction to adventure films proved highly popular. However, Hammer did have rivals in Britain, and the most notable of these companies was Amicus.

Amicus' portmanteau films included Dr. Terror's House of Horrors (1964), directed by genre stalwart Freddie Francis, Torture Garden (1967), The House That Dripped Blood (1970), Tales from the Crypt (1972), Asylum (1972), Vault of Horror (1973), From Beyond the Grave (1974), and The Monster Club (1980). These films typically feature four or sometimes five short horror stories, linked by an overarching plot featuring a narrator and those listening to his story.

Amicus took the same direction as their rival, Hammer Studios, in regard to occult theme anthologies and broadened the scope when it came to exploitation of women and Satanism within the framework of their films.

One of the most important branches of horror studios which emerged during 1960's Britain and which sparked a more mature theme when it came to violence and cult themed horror, was American International Pictures (AIP). A bridge between American investors and British directors, AIP began their productions on a series of films based on the works of Edgar Allen Poe. Directed by a young Roger Corman, and starring Vincent Price, AIP created more sadistic, cult driven films such as, "The Masque of the Red Death" and "The Tomb of Ligeia" (both 1964). Some contend that these productions paved the way for more explicit violence in both horror and mainstream films. It was obvious that horror films were not only big business, but were changing how audiences viewed subjects in a more tolerable climate. The more audiences as well as society began to accept the films that were coming out, not only in America, but also England, ideas about subjects such as witchcraft, black magic, Satanism and paganism began to become more accepting, more inviting and in most cases, "fun". The social stigmatism which for decades earlier was beginning to collapse and give way to a more liberal approach to the occult.

Chapter Seven
Cause and Effect

A recent U-M study regarding horror films and their initial effect on young people showed interesting data. The study showed that One in four college students in a recent study said they experience lingering effects of a frightful movie or TV experience from childhood. These effects range from inability to sleep, to avoidance of situations portrayed in those movies.

In their study "Tales from the Screen: Enduring Fright Reactions to Scary Media," U-M researcher Kristen Harrison and colleague Joanne Cantor of the University of Wisconsin found that 90 percent of the study's participants (more than 150 college students at Michigan and Wisconsin) reported a media fright reaction from childhood or adolescence. Moreover, about 26 percent still experience a "residual anxiety" today.

"This may not be surprising, but the proportion of participants--one in four--who reported fright effects that they were still experiencing indicates that these responses should be of major concern," says Harrison, assistant professor of communication studies. "These effects were more serious than jumpiness at a slammed door or the need to use a nightlight. They ranged from an inability to sleep through the night for months after exposure, to steadfast and continuing avoidance of the situations portrayed in the programs and movies."

The researchers, whose study will appear in a forthcoming issue of the journal Media Psychology, found that 52 percent of the sample reported disturbances in normal behavior such as sleeping or eating after viewing a frightening film or TV program. More than a third avoided or dreaded the depicted situation in their own lives, and nearly a fourth reported obsessive thinking or talking about the frightening stimulus.

While more than one-fourth of the study's participants still experience such aftermath, the duration of the effects--both past and present--range from less than a week (about 33 percent of the sample) to more than a year (about 36 percent).

According to the study, a wide range of symptoms were reported, including crying or screaming (27 percent of participants), trembling or shaking (24 percent), nausea or stomach pain (20 percent), clinging to a companion (18 percent), increased heart rate (18 percent), freezing or feeling of paralysis (17 percent) and fear of losing control (11 percent), as well as sweating, chills or fever, fear of dying, shortness of breath, feeling of unreality, dizziness or faintness, and numbness (all less than 10 percent each).

"It appears, then, that the physical and emotional fright reactions our sample experienced in reaction to media stimuli are very similar to those typically experienced in reaction to real-life stimuli, a finding that is consistent with the principle of stimulus generalization," Harrison says.

The most frequently reported type they found is blood/injection/injury (reported by 65 percent of the sample). One participant said that in the movie Jaws, it was not the shark or actual deaths that was frightening, but the blood.

"For about two months after the movie, I had nightmares about blood," the participant said. "The nightmares didn't always involve sharks, but always contained gross amounts of blood. To this day, I remain horrified of blood."

Harrison says that it is not clear whether this type of stimulus was mentioned most frequently because it is inherently more frightening than the other types, is the most common stimulus found in the mass media or, for some reason, is recalled more easily.

"In any case, the ubiquity of blood and gore in the U.S. media should be cause for concern regarding its potential for causing enduring fright reactions in children," she says.

Disturbing sounds/distorted images is the other most common type of fright stimulus found in films and TV programming (reported by 60 percent of participants). One participant was scared by the heavy breathing of the killer in the film Halloween, while several others found the suspenseful music in Jaws frightening.

The other three classes of stimuli were reported by a minority of the sample: situational (33 percent), animal (12 percent) and environmental (9 percent).

According to Harrison and Cantor, the younger the study's participants were when they viewed a scary movie and TV program, the longer-lasting the effects. In addition, their data provide little support for the popular notion that children who like thrilling media genres will be better able to handle their effects than children who do not like them.

Further, the average duration of fright effects for participants who watched frightening media because someone else was watching or wanted to watch was significantly higher than the duration for those who sought out the film or program themselves.

"The enduring fright reactions reported in this study were not the product of strange or unusual viewing circumstances," Harrison says. "Considering the abundance of graphically violent content in movies and on premium cable television channels, as well as the tendency for younger family members to go along with older members' media choices, it is not surprising that enduring fright effects from scary media were prevalent in our sample."

Finally, regardless of what frightened them as children, the study's participants appeared to know which coping strategies worked best for them, the researchers say. For example, those younger at exposure relied more heavily on behavioral coping strategies (covering their eyes, leaving the room, hugging a pillow), while those older at the time of viewing used cognitive strategies (reassuring oneself that "it's just a movie" or "this could never happen in real life").

"Many adults have learned to recognize the types of stimuli that frighten them and can choose movies and programs carefully to avoid such content," Harrison says. "Given that very young children may not yet know what types of stimuli frighten them most, and that they do not enjoy the power to choose which media the family will view, they are in special need of protection from exposure to such scary stimuli before coping strategies are necessary.

"It is reasonable to recommend that we pay closer attention to the potential media stimuli may have for creating long-lasting fears of the surrounding world, fears that can interfere with normal functioning. Given that normal functioning of children is an essential goal of child-rearing, parents should be aware of the types of media that may contribute to enduring fright effects in their children."

According to the film critic William K. Everson, the horror film is the most unique of any film genre because rigid guidelines do not have to be followed as closely by the director or, for that matter, the screenwriter. The horror film's message of terror and death can be subtly communicated to the audience or conveyed in very intense (and ultimately disturbing) visual and auditory cues. While other film genres might use restraint and logical explanation as their overriding criteria, the horror film need not follow this standard formula; thus, many cinematic tricks and techniques are available to filmmakers to employ at their discretion. The end result is that the audience can experience a wide range of negative effects, from minor irritation to overwhelming nausea, when viewing a film of the horror genre.

Based on Everson's remarks, one might conclude that the salient reason given as to why people watch horror films is that they want to be scared. In fact, this scare drive is so powerfully addictive to some viewers that they keep coming back to these films over and over again, desiring more terror and craving more thrills with each viewing.

When we look past the psychological aspects of horror films, when we look past the scary makeup, the ghostly castles or eerie mansions, when we get past the haunting images which make our heart beat faster with each fleeting step of the woman being chased by the monster, we begin to see something more taking place behind the horror film. We see a demonic spirit of influence taking place, and many are being lured into its seduction.

A 17 year old in the UK was murdered by three people who had kidnapped the young man, tied him to a tree, made him drink gasoline and then set him on fire. Their reasoning? They had watched the popular movie - "Saw" and wanted to act out the very scenes they saw depicted.

Another copy cat influence which came from horror film, "Saw" was one which shook many in law enforcement. Take the case of one Psychotic Benjamin Scott, 32, who slashed and stabbed his near neighbor Gary Beech at least 120 times in the eyes, head, face and back, after a petty argument. A drug addict inspired by the brutal Saw horror movies has been jailed indefinitely for the sadistic killing of a friend - just days after warning he would do 'something stupid' to return to prison.

Days before the brutal attack, Sheffield Crown Court heard how Scott - who had a history of mental illness and convictions for violence and robbery - had been admitted to a health facility as an in-patient for psychiatric treatment, but was discharged.

Police found at his apartment, the entire DVD series of the Saw films - which belong to a mini-genre of extreme horror films known as 'torture porn', where people are regularly imprisoned, mutilated and killed for little apparent reason.

Yet, the influences of horror films don't stop there. Here are eight horror movies that inspired real-life crimes:

1. Natural Born Killers

Natural Born Killers has inspired some of the most gruesome copycat killings in history. The film has been associated with several serial killers, including the homicidal couple Sarah Edmonson and Benjamin Darras. In 1995, the murderous duo dropped LSD and watched Natural Born Killers repeatedly before going on a drug-fueled crime spree of robbing and shooting a convenience store clerk that left her a quadriplegic. During the crime spree, Darras shot and killed a Mississippi businessman. Edmonson was sentenced to 35 years in prison and Darras is doing life.

2. Scream

Wes Craven's slasher movie series Scream was the inspiration behind the murder of Gina Castillo by her 16-year-old son and his 15-year-old cousin, Samuel Ramirez. The two teenagers confessed to the gruesome murder of Castillo and admitted that they did it because they needed money to fund a murder spree that would reenact the story line of the first two Hollywood Scream movies. In order to follow the Scream story line, the teenage boys planned to buy the ghost-face mask and electronic voice boxes that are seen in the movie.

3. A Clockwork Orange

Stanley Kubrick's A Clockwork Orange has been the inspiration for many twisted real-life crimes, specifically throughout Britain. The crimes have exhibited similarities with the film, but one of the most bizarre cases involved a man named John Ricketts who was dressed up as a droog from A Clockwork Orange and assaulted a woman dressed as Little Britain's Vicky Pollard at an office party. The violent movie was banned from UK cinemas because of the increase in violent crimes following its release.

4. Queen of the Damned

In 2002, Allan Menzies murdered his longtime friend, Thomas McKendrick, because he claimed a character in the vampire movie, Queen of the Damned, told him to do it and promised to make him a vampire in the next life. After watching the film about 100 times and receiving a visit from the female vampire Akasha in the middle of the night, he decided to murder people. Menzies also believed that McKendrick and another friend were plotting to kill him, but he turned on McKendrick first. Menzies stabbed his friend to death, drank his blood, and ate part of his head before burying him in a shallow grave. The "vampire killer" was later found dead in his prison cell from an apparent suicide.

5. Child's Play 3

Robert Thompson and Jon Venables were 10 years old when they kidnapped and brutally murdered two-year-old James Bulger in Liverpool. In 1993, Thompson and Venables snatched the toddler from a shopping mall and took him to a railway line where they beat and sexually assaulted the young boy. They left Bulger's mutilated body on the railway tracks to die. Thompson and Venables were supposedly inspired by the horror film Child's Play 3. The killer doll movies caused a great deal of controversy in the United Kingdom, as well as a public outcry for tightening "video nasties."

6. American Psycho

In 2004, Michael Hernandez, 14, stabbed his middle school classmate to death and admitted to modeling his behavior after the serial killers in American Psycho and The Silence of the Lambs. The South Florida teen said he identified with the horror movie murderers and wanted to act out their roles in his real-life plan to become a serial killer. Hernandez believed God gave him special powers and agreed with his decision to kill his classmate. The teen boy was found guilty of first-degree murder in 2008.

7. Nightmare on Elm Street

The famous '80s horror film, Nightmare on Elm Street, was the inspiration for Daniel Gonzalez's killing spree. In 2004, the paranoid schizophrenic went on a drug-fueled rampage and murdered four random people, including a doctor and his wife. Gonzalez armed himself with several knives and acted out a Freddy Krueger-like spree. Official reports claimed that Gonzalez did not receive proper treatment for his mental condition. He was given six life sentences for the four murders, as well as two attempted murders throughout England. In 2007, Gonzalez committed suicide in his cell.

8. Saw

The Saw horror movie series was the inspiration behind a cruel prank that turned into a serious matter for two teenage girls in Winchester, Tenn. The teenagers used the Saw plot of making victims play games to stay alive by leaving a gruesome message on 52-year-old Beverly Dickson's phone. They told Dickson that one of her friends was hidden in her house and it would be filled with toxic gas shortly. They asked if she wanted to live or die. Dickson got the message while attending a funeral and suffered a stroke from the frightening incident. The two 13-year-olds responsible for the prank call were charged with phone harassment.

Obviously the connections of violent inspired events in relationship to horror films are indisputable, yet, they are only but one aspect of the connection to horror films and inspired violence. Some horror films are based on real life events in which murder, rape, torture, or even Satanic occurrences took place.

I could probably spend the next 48 hours in connecting the dots of real life horrors which have inspired many modern horror films today. However, let me give you two significant events which have become cemented into our culture as relating to horror and the supernatural. When we look at real demonic influence creating the storyline for a well adapted film, we must not forget the spiritual connection.

When we think of "haunted" houses, no other structure comes to mind other than the popular Amityville house.

On November 13, 1974, police discovered six members of the DeFeo family -- father, mother and four of their five children -- shot and killed execution style at 112 Ocean Avenue in

Amityville, New York. By 1977, the DeFeo home would be the center of a haunted house story called the Amityville Horror.

In 1977, a runaway bestseller titled The Amityville Horror, written by Jay Anson, took the nation by storm. The promotional copies sent out by the publisher, Prentice Hall, hailed it as "the nonfiction Exorcist." The cover carried the subtitle of "A True Story," while the copyright page read: "The names of several individuals mentioned in this book have been changed to protect their privacy. However, all facts and events, as far as we have been able to verify them, are strictly accurate."

DeFeo Family

Ronald "Butch" DeFeo

George Lutz

Author Jay Anson undertook the daunting challenge of chronicling George and Kathleen Lutzes' claims that they and their three small children felt threatened from strong supernatural forces while living at 112 Ocean Avenue. Apparently, the family moved into the DeFeo house believing it to be their dream home.

On December 18, 1975, the Lutz family moved into the DeFeo home. Although it had only been 13 months since the DeFeo murders had occurred, the family later claimed at a press conference, "The DeFeo slayings weren't something that would bother us."

According to Anson's book, Father Mancusco arrived to bless the family's new home on the same day they moved into it. While the Lutzes unloaded their rented moving van, the Catholic priest entered the house and began his ritual blessing alone. He made his way upstairs to the second floor and entered the northeast bedroom, which had been Marc and John DeFeos' room.

As he sprinkled holy water around the room and recited a prayer, he heard a loud male voice allegedly say, "Get out!" Although the priest supposedly did not tell the family about the voice, he did warn them about the room, saying, "Don't use it as a bedroom. Don't let anyone sleep in there." According to a Good Housekeeping article, dated April 1977, the Lutzes followed the priest's advice, turning the room into a sewing room.

From the very first night they moved in, the family claimed they felt strange sensations. Anson had written that the family's personality had drastically changed. On one occasion in the book, the young couple beat their children with a strap and large wooden spoon. After moving to the house, the children apparently had become brats.

Purportedly, things worsened over the next few weeks. From the stench of bile to the smell of cheap perfume, the family became increasingly perplexed by the mysterious odors that would emanate from different locations of the house. Black stains appeared on the toilets and could not be lifted even with Clorox. Green slime ran down walls, although there appeared to be no reason or source. Hundreds of flies appeared in the sewing room despite it being the dead of winter. Of course, Anson's crowning moment was an upside down crucifix.

According to Anson, the phenomena then turned physical. Kathy was victimized by unseen touches, which had sometimes forced her to pass out. On the other hand, George would sit hours by the fireplace because he suffered from constant chills. In addition, he would wake up nightly at 3:15 a.m., reasoning that there was a connection between that hour and the hour the DeFeos were killed. In reality, the time of the deaths was never determined by the medical examiner.

As the month progressed, apparently the situation worsened again for the family. Anson reported that George awoke one night to witness his wife transform into a 90 year old hag. The next night, she began levitating off the bed, forcing her husband to grab her before she floated away.

Realizing they needed help, the family contacted the same Catholic priest to ask him to return to perform another blessing. According to Jay Anson's book, the priest had been feeling the aftereffects from the first blessing. Whatever was plaguing the family was also bothering the priest. (See the Catholic Church Speaks Out section.)

After failing to get the priest to return, the family took matters into their own hands. Armed with a crucifix, they walked throughout the house reciting the Lord's Prayer. A chorus of voices erupted in response, asking them, "Will you stop?"

The most incredible part of Anson's story was his claim that the daughter had befriended an invisible, red eyed pig named Jodie. "Jodie could not be seen by anyone unless it wanted to. At times it was a little bigger than a teddy bear and other times bigger than the house," George Lutz explained in October 1979 on the TV show "In Search Of," which he served as a consultant and participant for the show.

One night while coming back from the boathouse, Anson had George Lutz witnessing Jodie standing behind his stepdaughter in her bedroom. Kathy Lutz's introduction to her daughter's friend was just as disturbing. On a separate evening, she was startled to see two red eyes peering in through the darkness from the window. Although Anson's version was dramatic, Hollywood's adaptation was simply unbelievable.

The book reported that the malevolent forces caused significant property damage to the house, such as the front door being ripped off its hinges, windows being smashed, banisters being torn from their fittings, damage to the garage door, and water damage from hurricane force winds, which local meteorological stations had no record of.

Even their dog, Harry, a malamute Labrador mix, supposedly suffered from the strange forces. Although the animal was normally hyper, it had become increasingly lethargic while at the house. One time the dog had almost choked itself because it tried to scale the fence, or so the book would have readers believe.

One of the more chilling events in Anson's book was when George awakened to the sound of a marching band in his living room. He claimed he raced downstairs and entered the room, only to find dead silence and the furniture pushed to one side.

After 28 days in the DeFeo home, the family claimed they could take no more. They grabbed only a few belongings and fled the house, taking shelter at Kathy Lutz's mother's home in nearby Babylon.

Jay Anson's The Amityville Horror sold more than three million copies and was turned into a major motion picture that grossed more than $80 million dollars. The family happily went on a nationwide tour to promote the book as their "true story." Nevertheless, questions remained about the validity of their claims.

To this day, George Lutz (who has since passed away) maintained the real life inspired events were true, even though many critics dispute Lutz's belief as nothing more than tall tales spun over one evening with bottles of wine with his attorney trying to sell the story, the truth remains to be known, whatever took place within the quaint, northeastern Victorian home was based, in part, on demonic events, which I believe, when we examine the fact that Ronald DeFeo, Jr., who maintained his defense that his entire reasoning for taking a shotgun and systematically going to each room, at 3am in the morning, and blasting each member of his family, from his parents who were sleeping, to his young brother and sisters.

The fact remains, there is a genuine connection between ritualistic murders and their then depictions in a horror film. The truth is, the murders itself were Satanically inspired, the book was Satanically inspired, and ultimately, the movie itself, which has grossed over 1 billion and a slew of sequels which followed, not to mention numerous television programs which depicted the events inspired, are in fact Satanically inspired.

The second movie which has become part of our crave for horror films was the 1977 horror film - The Exorcist.

This popular movie tells the story of a young girl near Georgetown University who becomes the target of a malevolent spirit. The church is brought in, and an elderly, experienced exorcist, aided by a doubtful younger priest, comes to the family's aid. Although the reason for the possession is never given, it is suggested that an Ouija board contributed, although the spirits target is clearly the elderly priest, rather than the young girl.

The Exorcist was inspired by a 1949 case of demonic possession and exorcism that Blatty heard about while he was a student in the class of 1950 at Georgetown University, a Jesuit school. In January 1949, the family of 13-year-old "Robbie Doe" began to be disturbed by scratching sounds that came from inside of the walls and ceilings of the house. Believing that the house was infested with mice, the parents called an exterminator but he could find no sign of rodents. To make matters worse, his efforts seemed to add to the problem. Noises that sounded like someone walking in the hallway could be heard and dishes and objects were often found to be moved without explanation.

And while the noises were disturbing, they weren't nearly as frightening as when Robbie began to be attacked. His bed shook so hard that he couldn't sleep at night. His blankets and sheets were torn from the bed. When he tried to hold onto them, he was reportedly pulled off the bed and onto the floor with the sheets still gripped in his hands.

Those who have come to believe the boy was genuinely possessed feel that he may have been invaded by an invisible entity after experimenting with an Ouija board. He had been taught to use the device by his "Aunt Tillie", a relative who took an active interest in Spiritualism and the occult. Tillie had passed away a short time before the events began and it has even been suggested that it was her spirit who began to plague the boy. This seems unlikely though, especially considering the timing of her death. She lived in St. Louis and had died of multiple sclerosis on January 26, 1949 - a number of days after the phenomena surrounding Robbie began. However the family did feel there was some connection, as was evidenced in the written history of the mystery.

An alleged page from the exorcist diary -- "A Case Study by Jesuit Priests"

Many of the early events in the case were chronicled by the Jesuit priests who later performed the exorcism. Apparently, a diary was kept and it was the same diary that was heard about by author William Peter Blatty when he was a student at Georgetown University in 1949. He first became interested in the story after reading about in newspaper articles and discussed it with his instructor, the Rev. Thomas Bermingham, S.J.. The "diary" of the Robbie Doe case came to light in the fall of 1949 under rather odd circumstances. Father Eugene B. Gallagher, S.J., who was on the faculty of Georgetown, was lecturing on the topic of exorcisms when one of his students, the son of a psychiatrist at St. Elizabeth's Hospital in Washington, spoke of a diary that had been kept by the Jesuits involved in the Robbie Doe exorcism. Father Gallagher asked the psychiatrist, who may have been one of the professionals involved in the early stages of the case, for a copy of the diary and eventually received a 16-page document that was titled "Case Study by Jesuit Priests". It had apparently been intended to be used a guide for future exorcisms. Blatty asked to see a copy of the diary, but his request was refused.

He later turned back to newspapers for information about the case and discovered that one of them actually listed the name of the priest involved. His name was Rev. William S. Bowdern, S.J. of St. Louis. Bowdern refused to comment on the case for the newspaper reports, as priests who perform exorcisms are said to be sworn to secrecy. Blatty tried contacting him anyway but the priest refused to cooperate. Out of respect, Blatty changed the identity of the possession victim in his book to a young girl, but the exorcist of the novel remains an apparently thinly veiled portrait of Bowdern.

Father Bowdern passed away in 1983, never publicly acknowledging the fact that he was involved in the St. Louis case. He had talked with other Jesuits though and eventually these stories reached a man named Thomas Allen, an author and contributing editor to National Geographic. He managed to find one of the participants in the case, Walter Halloran, S.J., who was then living in a small town in Minnesota. Halloran was suspicious at first but he did admit that there had been a diary. But was it the diary that fell into the hands of Father Gallagher? Maybe or maybe not...

According to legend, the diary that Halloran had access to later turned up as a 26-page document of the case that was literally snatched out of the old Alexian Brothers hospital just before it was demolished, so where did the 16-page diary come from? And what happened to it? Accounts have it that Father Gallagher later loaned his 16-page diary to Father Brian McGrath, S.J., then dean of Georgetown University, in the spring of 1950. When Gallagher later tried to retrieve the diary, he was told that seven pages of the diary had been lost. Only nine of the 16 pages remained and they were only photocopies.

Horror films have a unique ability to change or influence an individual to either do things or think things that, for the most part, would never do. That is both the power and seduction of horror films. The events which took place at the house of the DeFeo's were a tragic one, yet it reminds us of this important truth, Demons are real. There is no question that there was a spiritual influence with Roland DeFeo, DeFeo himself has later admitted that he "heard" voices telling him to kill his family, this should not be disputed but understood.

Demonic influences are real, they are evil, and when permitted thru the means of such vehicles as horror films, Ouija boards, rock music or horror books, they each open the doorway to Satanic influence. The events which followed in the life Roland DeFeo, though heartbreaking for all involved, serves an example of the true nature of the spirit of this world, mastered by Satan himself. Never underestimate the intent and fortitude of the enemy, he desires to kill all and destroy as many people as he can, this makes him and his tactics dangerous and well worth noting. Though we as Christians have nothing to fear because of the cross, the unsaved world cannot say the same. They are subject to his desires and ultimately his evil plan.

The events which later occurred with the Lutz family are not at all uncommon and actually quite often occur when people are unwilling victims to the past tragic events. We do not truly understand the "why" *some* demonic spirits occupy a house or plot of land, such as a cemetery, yet what we do know is, many times there is a foreknowledge that we cannot see that they can, remember, demons are not fallen angels, they are past beings who entered into rebellion with Lucifer before the time of Adam that lived upon the earth during the first stage of creation.

Demons are bodiless beings, which give the reason why they desire to occupy a host, usually another human being, yet we know throughout history that Demons on occasion can and will, occupy an animal, yet in each course of events, it's not haphazard, it's for a reason. That is why what took place in the Lutz's home was not false or manufactured as some claim, but deliberate, deliberate by Satan for a greater purpose. Again, nothing is done in the supernatural without purpose or reason, everything happens as it was originally designed, then carried out.

Amityville Horror was designed for this reason, to create another pathway for people to be drawn into the world of the occult and the supernatural. The Amityville Horror was demonically orchestrated in the supernatural to lure people into the paranormal. This is why there is such a demand for the Amityville movies and books, this is equally the reason why, to this day, the original house cannot keep an owner, because of lingering spiritual activity. The only answer is Christ and a complete turning away from darkness.

The Witch of Endor.

There was a sorceress whose name is not given, that brought one man to his end. That man being Saul, the King of Israel. God had already spoken that he would bring Saul's kingdom to an end due to Saul's refusal to accept God's directives, he (God) would establish David as his King and Saul's reign would be over.

Saul sought out a woman of the dark arts to relay information that only someone with her insight and "gift" could do. Although Saul had previously banished all sorcerers and conjurers from his kingdom, his concern about the final outcome of Israel's battle against the Philistines caused him to seek the services of someone with "a familiar spirit."

When his servants told him of such a woman at Endor, he disguised himself and visited her that night. He asked her to conjure up the spirit of the prophet Samuel to tell his fortunes. When the woman reminded him of the law against practicing her art, he assured her that she would be protected. The woman accordingly conjured up a spirit identified by Saul as Samuel. The spirit informed Saul that he and his three sons would die in battle the next day and that the Israelites would fall to the Philistines.

Saul, along with his sons, did in fact die the following day, just as the witch had foresaw.

When we allow ourselves to become involved with the occult, whether it be through mediums, Ouija boards, horoscopes, even watching horror films, or the vast books they have inspired, that individual has willfully opened up the doorway to another world, a world which has only one directive - destruction. The conduit, which is the horror film, to the world of the supernatural is an open one, open for all who desire to be lost in his darkness, chained within its bleak, pitch blackness of evil and those who partake of its poison suffers the eventual effects.

Some years ago I was asked by a family to come and help with a strange and unique problem they were having at home. For the past several weeks, they had been experiencing events such as doors closing and opening, lights turning on or off without human involvement. Then the voices began to arrive. For many long evenings, these wonderful, Godly grandparents, were beginning to hear strange voices coming from different parts of the house. It seemed there was no help for peace for this family.

When I further inquired about when these things began to occur, the Grandmother explained that things started happening when their 15 year old granddaughter came to live with them. The young woman would involve herself with vampires, to be exact - "Twilight". For months, she would dress gothic, her main music was equally dark and, of course, her choice of movies was all horror films.

When her grandparents began to explain their situation, I knew in my spirit what was happening, they were literally under a spiritual attack, as a door had been opened to the spirit world and out of that door came demonic spirits. Having personally dealt with demons in the past, I went to their house where, upon entering, one could sense an overbearing sense of an evil presence. One of the things I have known when dealing with the demonic, is that Satan hates the word. When Satan tempted Jesus during Christ's time of 40 days of fasting in the wilderness, Satan would come to Jesus and twist the word, tempting him to submit his power and authority. However, Christ knew and understood the dynamics of Satan's ploy and rebuked him, with the word.

When we deal with demonic strongholds, the ability to fight the enemy is not through fleshly means but spiritual means by the word of God in the pulling down of those same demonic strongholds. When we meditate on the things of God, on the goodness of God and his word, we bring into captivity every thought, every fleshly desire, and every temptation. This is why Paul said that we wrestle not with flesh and blood, but against principalities, against powers, against the rulers of the darkness of this world, against spiritual wickedness in high places. (Eph.6:12)

Gathering both grandparents together for prayer, we rebuked the spiritual stronghold that had been allowed to come inside to torment this family, we rebuked and binded the demonic elements, commanding them in the authority given to us in Jesus name, to leave. Prayers cloths were placed in different areas of the house, especially in the young girl's room such as her shoes, under her mattress where she slept, even in the very pockets of her jackets. A hedge of protection was being built around this young woman Satan had desired and a battle was set to begin.

For several weeks I had not heard anything from the grandparents, almost a month had passed, when I got word from the grandfather, his excitement and overwhelming joy could be seen as he began to inform me that within one week, everything had stopped, the demonic manifestations had stopped, the voices ended, the overwhelming presence of evil was lifted and a joy had come back to this family unit. Furthermore, the young woman in question suddenly changed (I had informed the grandparents that under no circumstances they were to let her know what we had done) and her actions, her behavior, dress and interests, all changed. The power of God lifted this young woman out of the circumstances she was in and her life changed.

Just as these tragic and startling events have shown, many are counted as casualties in the spiritual war which is taking place throughout our nation, and, in many instances, across the globe where people involve themselves in things which are based on the occult, namely - horror films. God's word is very clear, we are not to have anything to do with the darkness of this world or of Satan's playthings, especially horror movies. Whether or not we know it, every time a person, saved or unsaved, partakes in watching a horror film, they are committing idolatry, their very actions are no different than Witches walking in a circle or a Satanist conjuring up demonic forces. When we allow ourselves to become involved in those things, those who are born again, literally are polluting their spirit man with the presence of Satan, this is why we must never open ourselves with the things of this world, even if they seem innocent and harmless, they are deadly to the soul.

The only solution is to remove every item which pertains to those things that are evil, this will both ensure the purity of the spiritual life of the believer, but it will equally secure the health and well being of the unbeliever, even if they do not understand the significance of how Satan operates, they will not be held prisoner to demonic powers. That is the power of God working in the lives of those who give him the latitude to work with and a testament to those who do not know the Lord of his ability to bring peace to a troubled soul.

Chapter Eight
The Late, Late Show

As I was growing up in the mid 70's, television was still growing by leaps and bounds, yet, still confined to a few channels. There was no cable channels, no HBO, no DVD's and most certainly, no 300 channels to choose from. To be honest, I can't remember a time growing up where me or my younger brother could turn to a channel past 30, from my fading memory from those days, we had only the main networks, ABC, CBS and NBC. There was still local or regional independent television stations, but those channels consisted of mainly local subjects, nothing what you would find on networks today.

During this time, there was not much in regard to late night entertainment but network programs such as "All in the Family", "Adam-12" or "Hogan's Heroes". Those programs were all fresh, new and reflecting the changing world we were living in. One also had late night talk, such as Johnny Carson and Merv Griffin. But what we did have, during those formable years growing up was the late, late show.

There was no such thing as syndication as we know it today, to tell you the truth, when most special programs, TV shows and interesting programs were created, and since digital tapes had not been invented yet, often times those same programs were usually taped over, until someone got the bright idea that maybe we should record these programs on Beta and save them for later use. Again, the idea of re-runs, except for the older programs, was simply not heard of.

One of the means of being indoctrinated at an early age that I remember was late night television and the most common means of being introduced to horror films as a child myself as well as most of America was the concept of the late night horror host.

Mixing light hearted humor, a cheesy backdrop set and make shift props which looked like someone's Halloween storage they kept for years in the attic, the horror hosts of late, late night television began to grow in several markets around the country, and they had a growing audience.

The first television horror host is generally accepted to be Vampira (Maila Syrjanieme Nurmi). The Vampira Show featured mostly low budget suspense films, as few horror films had yet been released for television broadcast. Despite its short 1954-1955 run, The Vampira Show set the standard format for horror host shows to follow. She was also the first to incorporate the standard of the usage of sex and sex appeal, sheer sexuality and a hint of lesbianism that spun off into another individual - Elvira.

Hosts were often plucked from the ranks of the studio staff. In the days of live television, it was not uncommon for the weather man or booth announcer to finish nightly news broadcast and race madly to another part of the soundstage for a quick costume change to present the evening's monster tale.

While a few early hosts like Zacherley and Vampira became the icons of this nationwide movement, most hosts were locals. The impact of these friendly ghouls on their young fans cannot be underestimated. The earliest hosts are still remembered with great affection today.

"Fright Night" is probably one of the most remembered and most loved movie showcase programs from the NY Metro area of all-time. Simply put, it was one of the most unique and versatile movie showcase programs of it's era as well as offering the widest variety of films of any "monster movie" showcase at the time.

By the mid to late 70's, FN was really a drive-in theater or midnight horror theater right in your own living room. Briefly, FN ran on WOR-TV Channel 9 from 1973 to 1987. Much of the credit for it's programming goes to Lawrence Casey who was the stations programming manager at the time.

FN ran the gamut from old Universal horrors to Mexican horrors to Euro-Horrors to flicks fresh from the Drive-In circuit. When FN first aired, it concentrated on the old Universal films before gradually shifting to more "notorious" fare. How it was done is anybodies guess but there were times when these more violent films aired with little or no cuts at all. FN's time slot shifted at various times from 12 Midnight to it's most popular 1AM slot right after wrestling to later on

1:30AM but for 15 years, it was a steady, welcome friend and a fixture of WOR's Saturday late night programming.

On Saturday, December 7, 1957, WBKB premiered a series called "Shock Theatre" at 10 pm. "Shock Theatre" was the perfect vehicle for an evening around the television set. After popping some fresh popcorn (remember this was way before microwave ovens), turning the lights down low- or off if you dared- the show would be begin with the title of the show appearing on the screen only to shatter like breaking glass revealing a laughing skeleton who beckoned the viewers to "come on in." That scene would segue into the familiar outside view of a haunted house and of course the thunder and lightning as the camera moved toward the only lit window.

As the camera zoomed in, you saw bars on the window. The next thing you knew you were in a dark and dismal cellar complete with moss covered stone walls.

CREATURE FEATURES was WGN-TV's entry and no serious concern for WFLD. Known for it's main title vignettes of Universal Studios classic horror movies set to the haunting guitars of Henry Mancini's theme from the film "Experiment In Terror". Across the country, from New York to middle America, late night television had something unique to offer the youth and even dads who enjoyed the occasional fright film. Of course in my home State of Indiana, we too had our host for horror - a character by the name of Sammy Terry.

In the early 1960's, WTTV's Bob Carter and producers developed the character of "Sammy Terry" as an on-air personality. A cloaked, pale-faced ghoul who rose from his coffin on Friday nights, laughed ominously and introduced Horror films as well as provides commercial-break entertainment. Renamed Nightmare Theater and with the banter mostly ad-libbed, the show and Carter's portrayal of "Sammy Terry" won him a large-scale following in the region, which allowed him to be ranked with other horror hosts of the era who operated out of much larger broadcast markets.

The still relatively new medium of television provided a means for classic films to generate revenue, and as part of that, Universal Studios packaged a set of more than fifty films as part of a "shock theater" package that was shown by many television stations across the country, usually as late-night fare. When WTTV purchased the set of films, which had been rejected by local CBS affiliate WISH-TV, Carter was chosen as the host of the new program. Carter's Shock Theater originally included only still photographs punctuated by voice-over narration during the commercial breaks.

Over time, the popularity of the voice-overs with viewers and sponsors inspired Carter and his producers to develop the character of "Sammy Terry" as an on-air personality—a cloaked, pale-faced ghoul who rose from his coffin on Friday nights, laughed ominously, introduced and occasionally berated the films, and provided commercial-break entertainment. Renamed Nightmare Theater and with the banter mostly ad-libbed, the show and Carter's portrayal of "Sammy Terry" won him a large-scale following in the region, which allowed him to be ranked with other horror hosts of the era who operated out of much larger broadcast markets.

Then along came Elvira. Cassandra Peterson was born on September 17, 1949, in Manhattan, Kansas and grew up in Colorado Springs. Becoming host of Movie Macabre in October 1981 at KHJ-TV, a Los Angeles station. As she ridiculed the many lousy grade-Z pictures that she hosted, Elvira didn't shy away to use self-parody, with many subtle and unsubtle play on words, raunchy jokes and allusions to her personal life (and her prodigious physique). Of course, this was helped by an outrageous and sexy costume, a different wig that the one known today, and a personality based on the "Valley Girl"-type popular at the time.

Elvira soon became not only a movie "siren", but she (Cassandra) became a popular figure in the final stages of late night television. With her seductive smile, the wink of an eye and her willingness to exploit her breasts and the rest of her body, Cassandra was the final ingredient through her TV. persona of Elvira, "mistress of the dark" to bring about the change needed to bring horror films, the glorification of sex, nudity and seduction to the forefront.

The advent of late night television, limited programming and the strong late night audiences for this type of material, literally opened the door for horror films to take root in American culture. It could be argued that had it not been for those late night programs in the early days of television, horror films, as we know them today, would have never gained near the popularity and fanfare it has today.

Growing up in that very generation myself, I contend that it was the mixture of late night television and the early development of entertainment which paved the path to allow horror films to take root in the hearts and minds of people everywhere. Whenever Satan needs an avenue to bring about change, he often uses the most innocent and seductive measures to do it. Using comedy, sex appeal and the lowering of Godly values, Satan was able to indoctrinate millions of impressionable teens and young adults toward horror films and brought many into bondage from the very affects they (horror films) were contaminated with. Like a disease which spreads by contact, horror films, through the usage of imagery which seemed harmless and innocent enough, polluted many with its evil.

Chapter Nine
Saturday Morning poison

There is another form of indoctrination which has been introduced to families nationwide, it is through this form of manipulation that has captured the heart of many children around the world, it is the cartoon.

By the age of two or three, most children regularly watch 26-33 hours of television each week. The average child has watched more than 45,000 murders, 75,000 images of alcohol, over 100,000 images which are sexual and more than half a million which are occult based.

Some believe that the thoughts of children can create their own virtual reality. This is part of a greater plan by those who, for whatever reason, deem it necessary to process images of a deeper aspect of human spiritualism and that is by and through the occult.

When the three networks realized how popular (as well as financial) creating programs directly relating to kids would become during the early 60's, it opened up another segment of viewers. This not only became popular with many parents, but, as previously stated, financially rewarding as well. But Satan is equally wise to the hearts of men, and while some programmers developed quality, educational programs that children could find entertaining and which parents could feel relatively easy about, there was also another avenue which the enemy used to bring the occult into the American household, and that was through cartoons.

The use of innocence such as the image of a lovable cartoon character, a "never never" land for a setting and bright colors as an added feature, are literally designed for one purpose, to introduce a child into opening their minds to the world of imagination and make believe. Who can forget the scene from the movie Willy Wonka and the Chocolate Factory, where Wonka opens the door to a world of magic and mystery. The scene I'm referring to is where Wonka and the small group of 10 walks past the giant door as he begins the enchanting song, "Pure Imagination".

The scene, however quaint and innocent it may appear, actually contains a more deeper, symbolic meaning, it is the symbolism of opening ones mind to the wonder and majestic possibilities of the unknown. This is the same, powerful tool cartoons use to relay certain messages, good or bad, it's a tool nonetheless.

During the 60's however, a clever and interesting series of children's programming began to appear, many reflecting the social or interests of the current culture, especially the hippie movement. During this experimental period ran several cartoon's which dealt with subjects such as witchcraft, black magic, ghosts and the after life. "Milton the Monster, Casper the Friendly Ghost, and The Adams Family."

Under great pressure by the "Action for Children's Television", many of the cartoons deemed too violent were canceled and a more toned down series of cartoon's all under the scope of (ACT) and the Parent committee, (a consumer group of concerned Parents), cartoons took a hard turn for a more simpler, innocent content for quality Children's entertainment. Several programs emerged, from The Flintstone's to The Archie's, cartoons began to reflect more of content more suitable for kids. Still, the one thing which did not get removed from the equation was occult themed content found in many of the developing cartoons. But it would be in 1969, under the creative team of William Hanna and Joseph Barbera, that things would change the way cartoons would deal with the supernatural, and it would be all because of a dog named Scooby.

"Scooby-Doo, Where are you?" Debuted on September 13th, 1969. A mixture of music reflecting with the real life changes of the times and a group of hippy cultured youth, along with their dog named Scooby-Doo who investigates haunted houses in their Mystery Machine, CBS approved production of the first series and a hit was soon born.

With elementary themes such as Wicca (witchcraft), Necromancy, Black Magic and sorcery, a crop of new animated series for children became more and more common among the networks, soon, occult themed children's cartoons became a staple in American households as a new generation was being groomed of the ways of the occult.

Scooby-Doo was the beginning of the worship of the occult. The inclusion of such topics as phantom's, witches, ghosts, mediums, vampirism and even paganism (which includes Satanism), opened up an entire generation to the occult, and most children, as expected, knew very little of the harm that these subjective teachings, through the use of animation, would condition them to begin to accept dark subjects.

As the nation progressed into the late 70's and early 80's, the culture began to change in its ideas and philosophies, many cartoons began to shift away from topics like those found in Scooby-Doo, however, even though the change was taking place, what didn't change was the growing appetite of the past generation(s) who remembered their childhood past time and wanted to keep their horror tradition.

By the end of 1979, horror films were finding a place with movie audiences, and most who were finding the current wave of horror films such as Halloween, Carrie and Friday the 13th, were the very children of the early 60's who, now young adult's, had grown accustomed to the occult and its evil. The enemy had positioned his deception in the heart of the children, and the children were now older and ready for more mature teachings of the occult.

Decades passed, the imagery and subsequent work that followed in the world of animation began to change, what was considered "new" and innovating in the late 60's had become dated and out of touch with the texting generation. By the 21st century, animation had taken on an entire new look, gone were the old penciled layered still frames used to create such lovable characters as Wild E Coyote and Bugs Bunny, in its place came a new form of animation - computer CGI.

Yet, with all of the obvious changes in appearance and content, the one thing which remained tried and true, was the use of the occult. The occult and its sordid history from pagan, Satanic roots has seemed to survive each passing decade, even an entire century, the occult has proven it has resistance to whatever time it faces, simply because it is rooted in a larger source and that source is Satan.

Gone were the days of Shaggy and the gang, now a new crop of animation has begun to flourish, many of which are heavily ladened with occult symbolism and rituals, some openly flaunting their occult roots. Characters such as teenage witches or teen wolfs occupy many television programs today.

But creators didn't stop at television, they began to look to the movie theater for a more bigger audience stake. During the late 90's and well into the 21st century, cartoons had all but been replaced by animation, a more rapid display of a sequence of images to create an illusion of movement, imagery which is usually created by computer generated software.

With the success of crossover films like the live action, "Scooby-Doo", producers began to see the trend of using the old to create a new. Tim Burton became a master at using occult symbolism in his dark, dreary tales, his greatest success with occult symbolism came in the 1993 animated film, "The Nightmare Before Christmas".

The Nightmare Before Christmas, tells the story of Jack Skellington, a being from "Halloween Town" who opens a portal to "Christmas Town" and decides to celebrate the holiday. Halloween Town is a dream world filled with citizens such as deformed monsters, ghosts, ghouls, goblins, vampires, werewolves and witches. Jack Skellington ("The Pumpkin King") leads them in a frightful celebration every Halloween.

The use of portals as a means of opening up one dimension which leads to another is called Astral projection. It is through this means which makes Burton's storytelling a dangerous one, not to mention the very fact that the setting of Burton's character - Jack, resides in a place called Halloween Town. Halloween, a pagan holiday by ancient practices by its own right, is the subject of a much more darker symbol of the occult, especially when used as a seductive instrument to lure children into the dark world of occult practices.

Several animated films as of late have sprung up that are, to some degree, even bolder in their obvious portrayal and involvement in the occult, two in particular, are ParaNorman and Hotel Transylvania.

ParaNorman, a Universal Pictures animated film, revolves around the life of an 11 year old boy, who is capable of not only seeing the dead, but communicating with them as well. To save his town from a witch and a rash of zombies, Norman seeks the help of the underworld of ghosts, ghouls and goblins. Norman is thought of as strange. In fact, the whole town rejects him because he talks to dead people. The story of PARANORMAN honors a dark supernatural world and the occult with a low budget stop-motion animation geared toward preteen children. It is through this means of bridging the gap between animation and the occult, combined with a unique figure (an 11 year old boy that many children can relate to) which makes ParaNorman a dangerous film for children to watch.

PARANORMAN has an underline message that it's OK to be different, even if that deals with talking to the dead. The one thing looked down upon is anger, putting pain upon people, and being unforgiving. Otherwise, however, the dark occult world is seen as OK to tamper with and to embrace.

Hotel Transylvania, the latest animated feature film and comedy actor, Adam Sandler, is the latest which openly deals with the occult but set around the theme of a classical haunted mansion and Count Dracula. Hotel Transylvania is the telling of an uninvited human who drops in on Count Dracula's secret hotel getaway for monsters and takes an interest in Dracula's daughter.

Hotel Transylvania confronts the concept of fearing those who are different. Humans are afraid of monsters, and the monsters are afraid of humans. They base their fears on assumptions made about each other. While this is a good message for children, it depicts monsters as misunderstood. In other words, it presents the villains as the victims.

God warns us to stay away from mediums, psychics, spirit communication, astral projection and divination for a reason. The spirit beings which empower these activities (or the people who practice them) are deceptive. They are fallen angels who disguise themselves up as "beings of light". What people glean from these spirits are the doctrines of demons, the twisting lies of familiar spirits, and a course which leads to destruction in the end.

The power of deception in regards to the occult, whether it be in a friendly ghost or an amusing dog, cannot be overlooked, or worse, ignored. Evil, even in small amounts, and in this case, sugar coated by the means of animated characters, funny catch lines and witty storytelling, set within the realm of a magical or Halloween setting, plays on the emotions of children as well as young adults. To make someone comfortable with something which is clearly wrong, the best method is to use humor and characters that make it more humanistic, more understandable which makes us sympathetic to the evil, when in reality we should not be sympathetic but resistant at every turn. How clever the enemy has become and how lazy we as Christians have become in dealing with such. Yet, the one outcome still remains the same, children are being indoctrinated into a world of the occult and most Parents are clueless about it, for many were fed the same sugary syrupy poison themselves and have no problem allowing their children to ingest the same.

If we are to break free from the clutches of the occult and its obvious influences upon our culture and society, then we need to make the necessary changes to what we allow ourselves to be apart of, even if it's difficult, even if it's not popular, the spiritual lives of our children are at risk and I believe well worth any negative pressure from those who see different.

Chapter Ten
Rocky's Perverted Horror Show

During the late 1960s and throughout the 70s, New York as well as many other Cities, especially the west coast, was riding the wave of rock musicals. Hair, Hairspray, Grease and of course Tommy, were finding receptive audiences worldwide. The success of this type of entertainment, reflective of the post hippie drug culture at the time, rock musicals were becoming popular and financially rewarding for all.

During this time, men such as Andrew Lloyd Webber and Tim Rice, were finding immediate success with "Jesus Christ Superstar", the rock musical concept was becoming an important part of the musical theatre scene throughout the 1970s, while fans were getting hooked on this new and popular mix of rock and roll and Broadway, and Satan began to add a new twist to the horror genre that would capture an entire subculture of young people to this day, and it would start with one British homosexual.

Richard Timothy Smith, better known thru his stage name, "Richard O'Brien", O'Brien would find himself engulfed with the world of Broadway, taking positions on such Broadway musicals such as "Jesus Christ Superstar" and "The Crystal Maze". It was during this pivotal time in 1973, O'Brien was about to release his only true mark of success, "The Rocky Horror Picture Show".

Taking cues from his own personal love for horror movies, Science Fiction films of the past and his personal obsession with homosexuality, O'Brien released this little known musical upon unsuspecting audiences in New York City. Within just a few short months, Rocky Horror had become an instant success with horror fans and a generation of free love, open minded young people who were not constrained by the morals and ethics of the past. Not without its set of critics who felt it did not live up to the typical musical fare, Rocky Horror did find its way into the hearts of people who liked the strange and the weird. It also found a segment of society who, by their own nature, was beginning to make waves into mainstream society with their own sexuality, namely, homosexuals.

In 1975, Rocky Horror would take the next major step in its strange and twisted version of abomination through the means of a motion picture. On August 14th, 1975, "The Rocky Horror Picture Show" opened up to movie audiences in nearly 40 markets across the U.S. Little did O'Brien or his financial backers would realize just how much of a success they would have until the film began a midnight run at the Waverly Theater in New York on 1 April 1976. The movie not only garnered major success, even greater than its original 75 opening, the movie literally did what no other "horror" film or musical of its kind has done since, it became a cult phenomenon.

So what is The Rocky Horror Picture Show? The concept, although less appealing in its description, centers around the lives of two main characters, a newly-engaged couple Brad Majors and Janet Weiss, who find themselves lost and with a flat tire on a cold and rainy late November evening. Seeking a phone with which to call for help, Brad and Janet walk to a nearby castle, where they discover a group of strange and outlandish people who are holding an Annual

Transylvanian Convention. They watch as the Transylvanians, servants and a tap-dancing groupie dance the film's signature song, "Time Warp".

They are soon swept into the world of Dr. Frank-N-Furter, a self-proclaimed "Sweet Transvestite" from Transsexual, Transylvania. The ensemble of convention attendees also includes servants Riff Raff, his Magenta, and a groupie named Columbia.

Frank claims to have discovered the "secret to life itself". His creation, Rocky Horror, is brought to life. The ensuing celebration is soon interrupted by Eddie, an ex-delivery boy, partial brain donor to Rocky, and Columbia's lover, who rides out of a deep freeze on a motorcycle. In a jealous rage, Frank corners him and kills him with an ice axe. He then departs with Rocky to a bridal suite off of the laboratory.

Brad and Janet are shown to separate bedrooms where each is visited and seduced by Frank, who poses as Brad and then Janet. Janet, upset and emotional, wanders off to look for Brad, who she discovers, via a television monitor, is with Frank. She then discovers Rocky, cowering in his birth tank, hiding from Riff Raff, who has been tormenting him. While tending to his wounds, Janet becomes intimate with Rocky, as Magenta and Columbia watch from their bedroom monitor.

After discovering that his creation is missing, Frank, Brad and Riff Raff return to the lab, where Frank learns that an intruder has entered the building. Dr. Everett Scott, Brad and Janet's old high school science teacher, has come looking for his nephew, Eddie, but Frank suspects that Dr. Scott investigates UFOs for the government. Upon learning of Brad and Janet's connection to Scott, Frank suspects them of working for him. Frank, Dr. Scott, Brad, and Riff Raff then discover Janet and Rocky together under the sheets in Rocky's birth tank, upsetting Frank and Brad.

Rocky and the guests are served dinner, which they soon realized has been prepared from Eddie's mutilated body. Janet runs screaming into Rocky's arms and is slapped and chased through the halls of the castle by a jealous Frank. Janet, Brad, Dr. Scott, Rocky and Columbia all meet in Frank's lab, where Frank captures them with the Medusa Transducer, transforming them into statues. They are then forced to perform a live cabaret floor show and have a semi-orgy in the pool (except Dr. Scott, who is stuck in his wheelchair), with Frank as the leader.

The performance is interrupted by Riff Raff and Magenta, who stage a coup and announce their plan to return to the planet of Transsexual in the galaxy of Transylvania. In the process, they kill Columbia, Rocky and Frank. They release Brad, Janet and Dr. Scott, and then depart by lifting off in the Castle itself.

The narrator then finishes the film by concluding that the human race is equivalent to insects crawling on the planet's surface.

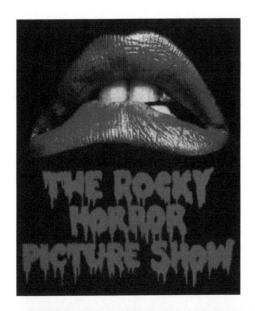

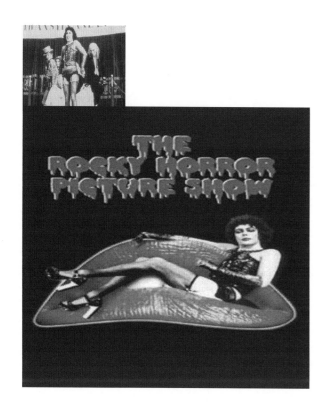

Since its initial 75 opening, The Rocky Horror Show has literally gone on to become a hit with decades of new audiences, especially young people. The concept of mixing traditional horror content, rock music, sex, and homosexuality, the movie as well as the musical has become a success every Halloween season. Yet, is there a seduction behind the phenomenon? Yes, not only a seduction of the glorification of the occult, but even worse, a celebration of perversion thru the ties to homosexuality. But this is the plan of the enemy, to glorify not only the horror genre, but something which is even worse - the gay lifestyle. Is it any great wonder that O'Brien knew this when he created Rocky Horror along the lines of a gay and transsexual storyline, when in reality he himself lived the same sordid lifestyle? Richard has claimed to dislike sexual labels, refusing to refer to himself as straight, gay, or bi. At a 2007 charity auction, he declared that "I have slept with 300 women, 30 or 40 men and around 12 transsexual's".

Homosexual Symbolism

Brad and Janet witness the "Transylvanians" (from Transsexual, Transylvania…an obvious homosexual reference), doing the "Time Warp", an obviously Satanic dance, as evidenced by it's orgiastic content ("pelvic thrust") and circles of doom.

"Frankenfurter" plays God, by creating his own personal sexual toy, a blonde haired man named Rocky. Rocky is a fine muscular specimen, but no man should lie with another man in bed. Yet this is what Frankenfurter plans for Rocky. Later in the film, Rocky plays with Janet's breasts while she sings "touch me I want to be dirty", while Frankenfurter does his sinful deeds to Brad in a pink room, initially posing as Janet but later giving Brad what appears to be oral sex.

The film shows constant gay pride references such as rainbows and speakers mounted on Greek statues of naked males. The film also shows a man lying with another man. The film also shows a man taking God's place by creating another man. The film also mocks the Sacred, Holy vow of Marriage.

Audience Participation

One of the ploys used throughout the movie and its midnight showings across the nation and in other parts of the world, is the campy, over the top audience participation that takes place in these screenings. From crowds shouting out the onscreen lines from obvious memorizations, to overtly sexual overtones throughout these settings, something of an obscene movement are taking place in many a young people's lives, and the only result is spiritual bondage.

First, every single viewer is slapped with a sexual toy, a "dildo" as their "virginity" is symbolically taken away. This is a clearly Satanic ritual.

Second, viewers scream obscenities at the film throughout the film in an organized, ritualistic fashion. This clearly shows the Satanic nature of the film. And yes, Janet might be a "slut", but do we really need to hear it every time her name is mentioned?

Third, people throw food around the theater, wasting valuable rice and toast and hot dogs that would serve a far better purpose in the bellies of our poor.

Fourth, people actually DRESS UP as these characters! There are numerous men in drag at every showing, making the theater itself a homosexual breeding ground of orgies and sin. Do you really want to be caught up in this mess?

Fifth, people actually engage in the "Time Warp". They do this Satanic dance as one large Satanic group. This is clearly sinful. Don't they know that there is only One True God, and that God is the True God, and not Satan?

Why is Tim Curry in drag? Why does Rocky play with the breasts of a woman who is engaged to be married? Why does "Riff Raff" have "elbow sex" with his sister? Why do Brad and Janet run around in their underwear? Why do the stars in the film practice ritualized cannibalism on screen? Why does everyone in the film wear lingerie? Why is there Satanic dancing? Why are there orgiastic homoerotic overtures throughout the film? The answer is clear. The Rocky Horror Picture Show, like every other horror film before it as well as after it, was inspired by none other than Satan himself.

Chapter Eleven
Creators of evil things

There are some combinations which just simply go together, bacon and eggs, burgers and fries, Burns and Allen. While most have a genuine appeal for what their unique combination has to offer, what goes well for food and Broadway is equal to the world of horror.

Horror novels are the lifeblood of horror movies and visa versa. Many of today's popular horror movies are or were in fact based off of a horror novel. From the dark works of Edgar Allen Poe and H.P. Lovecraft, to more contemporary writers such as Anne Rice and Stephen King, the horror novel is the heart of horror movies which beats the spirit of darkness throughout its long dark veins of terror.

Edgar Allan Poe

Edgar Allan Poe was born January 19th, 1809 in Boston Massachusetts. Poe was an American poet, author and literary critic. In January 1845 Poe published his poem, "The Raven", to instant success, bringing with it a vast history of writings, but equally a history of violence and personal failures with Poe's own personal life.

Poe had a profound impact on horror films when the medium began to flourish in the 20th century. From directors to screenwriters, Poe's dark work of macabre and morbid imagination produced a work which was both haunting as well as alluring to the reader. There was a sense of erotic seduction with many of his characters, some could say that a subtle hint of necrophilia to his work. His ability to combine grim and ghastly visualizations within the structure of a literary piece was superb.

His most recurring themes deal with questions of death, including its physical signs, the effects of decomposition, concerns of premature burial, the reanimation of the dead, and mourning. Many of his works are generally considered part of the dark romanticism genre, a literary reaction to transcendentalism, which Poe strongly disliked. He referred to followers of the movement as "Frog-Pondians" after the pond on Boston Common and ridiculed their writings as "metaphor-run mad," lapsing into "obscurity for obscurity's sake" or "mysticism for mysticism's sake." Poe once wrote in a letter to Thomas Holley Chivers that he did not dislike Transcendentalists, "only the pretenders and sophists among them."

Poe's personal life was equally grim, almost mirroring the very stories he created. A life of deep, dark depression surrounded him like a heavy mist and at times, a spirit of death walked with each step he took. His father abandoned their family in 1810, and his mother died a year later from consumption (pulmonary tuberculosis). Poe was then taken into the home of John Allan, a successful Scottish merchant in Richmond, Virginia, who dealt in a variety of goods including tobacco, cloth, wheat, tombstones, and slaves. The Allans served as a foster family and gave him the name "Edgar Allan Poe", though they never formally adopted him.

Even while young, Poe had a profound out look upon life, death and, ultimately, the after life. A deist at heart which would eventually lead him into the dark world of the occult when he was older, Poe became very acute to the idea which said that life was one of chance, a mere spin of the cosmic wheel and one's fate in life, to be rich or poor, sick or well, happiness or sadness, weighed in the balance.

His elder brother Henry, who had been in ill health in part due to problems with alcoholism, died on August 1, 1831. This would be followed by the death of his wife, Virginia due to tuberculosis. Poe began to drift further into alcoholism and his work, which would bring about a chance meeting, when returning back to America from Europe where Poe had sought refuge from the chaos and disorder found in his personal life, he met with one "Harley Warren", an occultist.

There are questions surrounding if "Warren" was indeed a real individual or one conjured up by H. P Lovecraft to protect the true identity of this particular occultist who became friends with and encouraged Poe's interest into the occult. Either way, Poe became very astute in matters of black magic, conjuring and spirit divination which eventually influenced many of Poe's literary work.

During much of Poe's life, his influence into the world of the occult, gothic fantasy with overtones of sexuality, all indicate someone who had become "anointed" in the art of storytelling in such a way which not only introduced the reader into forbidden subjects like mysticism and Witchcraft, but equally celebrated the dark aspects of the demonic spirit world Poe subscribed to. There is no question, in this author's mind that Edgar Allan Poe was a pawn of Satan to condition a future society into the affairs of demonic strongholds. Further more, it is beyond reasonable doubt, when we look at the trials and tribulations which surrounded Poe and his turbulent life, his drug addiction, the early deaths of those around him as well as the many occult symbolisms found in his work, it makes the case very solid to say that Edgar Allan Poe was a man lost, bound to demonic influence and oppression, and in some cases, I believe, possession.

We must understand that when a person lives their life without Christ, when someone walks their entire life without the shed blood of Jesus being applied to their soul, they are bound to the sins of this world, and worse, they are subject to the god of this world, which is Satan. Poe, in my estimation, was nothing more than a fixture of a man oppressed by the enemy, influenced by demonic spirits, hopelessly bound to sin without any hope, any recourse other than eternal destruction. As of late, there is no evidence Poe ever repented at the end of his life, yet, his work has carried on inspiring, influencing thousands into the world of the occult and Satanic ritual.

On October 3, 1849, Poe was found on the streets of Baltimore delirious, "in great distress, and... in need of immediate assistance", according to the man who found him, Joseph W. Walker. He was taken to the Washington College Hospital, where he died on Sunday, October 7, 1849, at 5 a.m..

Poe was never coherent long enough to explain how he came to be in his dire condition, and, oddly, was wearing clothes that were not his own. Poe is said to have repeatedly called out the name "Reynolds" on the night before his death, though it is unclear to whom he was referring.

Some sources say Poe's final words were "Lord help my poor soul." All medical records, including his death certificate, have been lost. Newspapers at the time reported Poe's death as "congestion of the brain" or "cerebral inflammation", common euphemisms for deaths from disreputable causes such as alcoholism. The actual cause of death remains a mystery, but this we can be assured, the Bible says, "Be sure your sins will find you out." (Numbers 32:33)

When a person rejects the cross, what Christ did on the cross (our atonement), they willfully rejects God's salvation and forfeit their claim to Heaven, equally so, they in turn allow Satan to do as he pleases within the confines of God's supreme direction and permission, and, at will, can claim that soul for damnation. Unless Poe cried out to God for mercy and repented, he is lost and even today, is dwelling in that place called Hell for eternity, until the judgment.

H.P. Lovecraft

Howard Phillips Lovecraft was born on August 20, 1890 in his family home in Providence, Rhode Island. Lovecraft was frequently ill as a child. Due to his sickly condition, he barely attended school until he was eight years old, and then was withdrawn after a year. He read voraciously during this period and became especially enamored of chemistry and astronomy. He produced several hectographed publications with a limited circulation beginning in 1899 with The Scientific Gazette. Four years later, he returned to public school at Hope High School (Rhode Island).

Bram Stoker

Edgar Allen Poe

Lovecraft

Anne Rice

Stephen King

Beginning in his early life, Lovecraft suffered from night terrors, a rare parasomnia disorder; he believed himself to be assaulted at night by horrific "night gaunts." Much of his later work is thought to have been directly inspired by these terrors. (Indeed, "Night Gaunts" became the subject of a poem he wrote of the same name, in which they were personified as devil-like creatures without faces.) It's interesting to note that Lovecraft's own Father, Winfield Scott Lovecraft, suffered from psychotic episodes which left him in a dehabilitated state at times.

Lovecraft wrote some fiction as a youth, but from 1908 until 1913, his output was primarily poetry. During that time, he lived a hermit's existence, having almost no contact with anyone but his mother. This changed when he wrote a letter to The Argosy, a pulp magazine, complaining about the insipidness of the love stories of one of the publication's popular writers, Fred Jackson.

The ensuing debate in the magazine's letters column caught the eye of Edward F. Daas, President of the United Amateur Press Association (UAPA), who invited Lovecraft to join them in 1914. The UAPA reinvigorated Lovecraft and incited him to contribute many poems and essays.

In 1917, at the prodding of correspondents, he returned to fiction with more polished stories, such as "The Tomb" and "Dagon". The latter was his first professionally-published work, appearing in W. Paul Cook's The Vagrant (November, 1919) and Weird Tales in 1923. Around that time, he began to build up a huge network of correspondents. His lengthy and frequent missives would make him one of the great letter writers of the century. Among his correspondents were Robert Bloch (Psycho), Clark Ashton Smith, and Robert E. Howard (Conan the Barbarian series).

In 1919, after suffering from hysteria and depression for a long period of time, Lovecraft's mother was committed to Butler Hospital just as her husband had been. Nevertheless, she wrote frequent letters to Lovecraft, and they remained very close until her death on May 24, 1921, the result of complications from gall bladder surgery.

As Lovecraft grew older and more educated in the world around him, he became interested in the occult. Like Stoker and Poe before him, Lovecraft seemed drawn to the mystical and dark influences of black magic and the supernatural. It was this interest in the occult itself that became a direct influence in Lovecraft's writings.

The central theme in most of Lovecraft's works is that of forbidden knowledge. Some critics argue that this theme is a reflection of Lovecraft's contempt of the world around him, causing him to search inwardly for knowledge and inspiration. In Lovecraft's works the search for forbidden knowledge drives many of the main characters. In most of his works this knowledge proves Promethean in nature either filling the seeker with regret from what they have learned, destroying them psychically, or completely destroying the person who holds the knowledge.

The beings of Lovecraft's mythos often have human (or mostly human) servants; Cthulhu, for instance, is worshipped under various names by cults amongst both the Eskimos of Greenland and voodoo circles of Louisiana, and in many other parts of the world.

These worshippers served a useful narrative purpose for Lovecraft. Many beings of the Mythos were too powerful to be defeated by human opponents, and so horrific that direct knowledge of them meant insanity for the victim. When dealing with such beings, Lovecraft needed a way to provide exposition and build tension without bringing the story to a premature end. Human followers gave him a way to reveal information about their "gods" in a diluted form, and also made it possible for his protagonists to win paltry victories. Lovecraft, like his contemporaries, envisioned "savages" as closer to supernatural knowledge unknown to civilized man.

When it came to religion, Lovecraft remained firm that he was anything but a believer. Lovecraft himself adopted the stance of atheism early in his life. In 1932 he wrote in a letter to Robert E. Howard: "All I say is that I think it is damned unlikely that anything like a central cosmic will, a spirit world, or an eternal survival of personality exist. They are the most preposterous and unjustified of all the guesses which can be made about the universe, and I am not enough of a hair-splitter to pretend that I don't regard them as arrant and negligible moonshine. In theory I am an agnostic, but pending the appearance of radical evidence I must be classed, practically and provisionally, as an atheist."

The Cthulhu Mythos of the Old Gods with Unspeakable names is evoked and worshipped, and respected practitioners of the esoteric use the symbolism and mythos as the basis of a magical system. Lovecraft had a remarkable insight into the occult and Satanism to such a degree that it is only reasonable to suggest that Lovecraft either was a member of a secret order, or was influenced by such members. Either way, as we'll examine in this writing, Lovecraft was more than just an imaginative writer and storyteller, he was an influencer of occult ideas and a prophet of things to come, especially his work which inspired many horror films in our present time.

One of the primary ceremonial magicians of the 'magical revival' that started in 19th Century England was Aleister Crowley, whose doctrines and practices are now often synthesized with the Cthulhu Mythos. Crowley would go on to become fluent in the occult and its practices, which leads us to his connection to Lovecraft. Lovecraft was an atheist, however, that being said, his (Lovecraft) notion of God, (referring to Christianity) was the basis of his rejection of Christ or anything remotely connected to Jesus Christ and the Bible. Lovecraft however, became a full follower of pagan gods and beliefs, which directly refutes his original claim that he maintained an antagonist belief system.

In 1918, Aleister Crowley was in New York. While there trying to establish his literary career, he met Sonia Greene. For many months, they (Crowley and Greene) would meet on an irregular basis for some time and became lovers. Still, this relationship would not last.

In 1921 Sonia Greene met the novelist H.P. Lovecraft, and in that same year Lovecraft published the first novel where he mentions Abdul Alhazred ("The Nameless City"). In 1922 he first mentions the Necronomicon ("The Hound"). On March 3rd. 1924, H.P. Lovecraft and Sonia Greene married.

It must be understood that during this time, Lovecraft's influences around him, had no doubt a great influence on his work. Being married, (many suggest Lovecraft, like Crowley, was a homosexual, or bi-sexual himself) his marriage to Sonia Greene was a short one, yet her influence on Lovecraft by her influences with Crowley, suggested that the ties of the circle of the occult was always surrounding Lovecraft which causes one pause to the work that came out of the mind of H.P. Lovecraft.

Some of Lovecraft's work was inspired by nightmares of his own. As he studied many scientific advances of biology, astronomy, geology, and physics, Lovecraft was more and more confounded and fueled his skepticism on humanity. His interest started from his childhood days when his grandfather would tell him Gothic horror stories. The influence of Arthur Machen, with his carefully constructed tales concerning the survival of ancient evil into modern times in an otherwise realistic world and his beliefs in hidden mysteries which lay behind reality, looms large.

Lovecraft was also influenced by authors such as Gertrude Barrows Bennett (who, writing as Francis Stevens, impressed Lovecraft enough that he publicly praised her stories and eventually "emulated Bennett's earlier style and themes"), Oswald Spengler, Robert W. Chambers (writer of The King in Yellow, of whom Lovecraft wrote in a letter to Clark Ashton Smith: "Chambers is like Rupert Hughes and a few other fallen Titans — equipped with the right brains and education but wholly out of the habit of using them").

The biggest influence was Edgar Allan Poe. Lovecraft had many similarities with Poe; they lost their fathers at a young age, loved poetry, and used archaisms (language pertaining to an earlier generation) in their writing. They both went against the contemporary styles and created their own worlds of fantasy.

Furthermore, Lovecraft's discovery of the stories of Lord Dunsany with their pantheon of mighty gods existing in dreamlike outer realms, moved his writing in a new direction, resulting in a series of imitative fantasies in a 'Dreamlands' setting.

In 1936, Lovecraft was diagnosed with cancer of the small intestine,[14] and he also suffered from malnutrition. He lived in constant pain until his death on March 15, 1937, in Providence. H. P. Lovecraft is now noted as a significant figure in 20th-century horror fiction. His writing, particularly the so-called Cthulhu Mythos, has influenced fiction authors worldwide, and Lovecraftian elements can be found in novels, films, movies, music, video games, comic books (e.g. the use of Arkham Insane Asylum in The Batman comic book series), and even cartoons.

Many modern horror and fantasy writers, including Stephen King, Bentley Little, Joe R. Lansdale, Alan Moore, Junji Ito, F. Paul Wilson, Brian Lumley, Caitlín R. Kiernan, and Neil Gaiman, have cited Lovecraft as one of their primary influences. Beyond direct adaptation, Lovecraft and his stories have had a profound impact on popular culture and have been praised by many modern writers.

Some influence was direct, as he was a friend, inspiration, and correspondent to many of his contemporaries, such as August Derleth, Robert E. Howard, Robert Bloch and Fritz Leiber. Many later figures were influenced by Lovecraft's works, including author and artist Clive Barker, prolific horror writer Stephen King, comic's writers Alan Moore, Neil Gaiman and Mike

Mignola, film directors John Carpenter, Stuart Gordon, and Guillermo Del Toro, horror manga artist Junji Ito, and artist H. R. Giger.

The impact of Lovecraft's work is directly related to his personal as well as relationship to the occult, his close ties to Aleister Crowley and his direct influences with subjects like the Necronomicon, the "Old Ones", which were nothing more than actual demons or even possibly fallen angels themselves. Lovecraft, like Poe, like Stoker, was nothing more than a pawn in a Satanic chess game to deceive many with a lie.

Stephen King

It has been said, and rightly so, that by far, the most influential name among horror writers, the one who can claim supremacy over past literary writers from Poe, Stoker and Lovecraft, to the present, is Stephen King. The body of his works is gripping, his craft of storytelling is compelling and how he has incorporated imagery of the darkness featured in much of his novels seem to have a life of its own, drawn from a source far greater than typical imagination can conjure up. His influences on film, television and the many who are guided by his work are daunting. King sits upon his throne as the "King" of horror - and with good reason, no other can claim his title. If ever there was one man with a "dark anointing" it is in fact Stephen King.

Stephen Edwin King was born September 21, 1947, in Portland, Maine. When King was two years old, his father left the family under the pretense of "going to buy a pack of cigarettes", leaving his mother to raise King and his adopted older brother, David, by herself, sometimes under great financial strain. The family moved to De Pere, Wisconsin, Fort Wayne, Indiana and Stratford, Connecticut. When King was eleven years old, the family returned to Durham, Maine, where Ruth King cared for her parents until their deaths. She then became a caregiver in a local residential facility for the mentally challenged.[1] King was raised Methodist.[14]

As a child, King apparently witnessed one of his friends being struck and killed by a train, though he has no memory of the event. His family told him that after leaving home to play with the boy, King returned, speechless and seemingly in shock. Only later did the family learn of the friend's death. Some commentators have suggested that this event may have psychologically inspired some of King's darker works,[15] but King makes no mention of it in his memoir On Writing.[16]

King's primary inspiration for writing horror fiction was related in detail in his 1981 non-fiction Danse Macabre, in a chapter titled "An Annoying Autobiographical Pause". King makes a comparison of his uncle successfully dowsing for water using the bough of an apple branch with the sudden realization of what he wanted to do for a living.

While browsing through an attic with his elder brother, King uncovered a paperback version of an H. P. Lovecraft collection of short stories entitled The Lurker in the Shadows that had belonged to his father. The cover art—an illustration of a yellow-green Demon hiding within the recesses of a Hellish cavern beneath a tombstone—was, he writes, the moment in his life which "that interior dowsing rod responded to." King told Barnes & Noble Studios during a 2009 interview, "I knew that I'd found home when I read that book."

From 1966, King studied English at the University of Maine, graduating in 1970 with a Bachelor of Arts in English. That same year his first daughter, Naomi Rachel, was born. He wrote a column for the student newspaper, The Maine Campus, titled "Steve King's Garbage Truck", took part in a writing workshop organized by Burton Hatlen,[2] and took odd jobs to pay for his studies, including one at an industrial laundry. He sold his first professional short story, "The Glass Floor", to Startling Mystery Stories in 1967.[1] The Fogler Library at the University of Maine now holds many of King's papers.

After leaving the university, King earned a certificate to teach high school but, being unable to find a teaching post immediately, initially supplemented his laboring wage by selling short stories to men's magazines such as Cavalier. Many of these early stories have been published in the collection Night Shift. In 1971, King married Tabitha Spruce, a fellow student at the University of Maine whom he had met at the University's Fogler Library after one of Professor Hatlen's workshops.[2] That fall, King was hired as a teacher at Hampden Academy in Hampden, Maine. He continued to contribute short stories to magazines and worked on ideas for novels.[1] It was during this time that King developed a drinking problem, which would plague him for more than a decade.

In 1973, King's novel Carrie was accepted by publishing house Doubleday. King threw an early draft of the novel in the trash after becoming discouraged with his progress writing about a teenage girl with psychic powers. His wife retrieved the manuscript and encouraged him to finish it.[22] His advance for Carrie was $2,500, with paperback rights earning $400,000 at a later date. King and his family moved to southern Maine because of his mother's failing health. At this time, he began writing a book titled Second Coming, later titled Jerusalem's Lot, before finally changing the title to 'Salem's Lot (published 1975). In a 1987 issue of The Highway Patrolman magazine, he stated, "The story seems sort of down home to me. I have a special cold spot in my heart for it!"[23] Soon after the release of Carrie in 1974, his mother died of uterine cancer. His Aunt Emrine read the novel to her before she died. King has written of his severe drinking problem at this time, stating that he was drunk delivering the eulogy at his mother's funeral.

After his mother's death, King and his family moved to Boulder, Colorado, where King wrote The Shining (published 1977). The family returned to western Maine in 1975, where King completed his fourth novel, The Stand (published 1978). In 1977, the family, with the addition of Owen Phillip (his third and last child), traveled briefly to England, returning to Maine that fall where King began teaching creative writing at the University of Maine. He has kept his primary residence in Maine ever since.

In 1985 King wrote his first work for the comic book medium, writing a few pages of the benefit X-Men comic book Heroes for Hope Starring the X-Men. The book, whose profits were donated to assist with famine relief in Africa, was written by a number of different authors in the comic book field, such as Chris Claremont, Stan Lee, and Alan Moore, as well as authors not primarily associated with that industry, such as Harlan Ellison.

Occultist themes and pagan religions have all influenced King throughout his vast span as a prolific writer of the horror genre, but one man stood among all the others who influenced King most, and that was none other than H.P. Lovecraft.

King has stated many times of Lovecraft's influence upon him as a young boy, from Lovecraft's early work, to many of his more popular titles which came later in his career, King took great interest from these early works of occultist ramblings which actually nurtured King's own interest in the occult and the supernatural.

Stephen King's books as well as movies are occultist because they reject the tenants of the Christian faith. King himself an agnostic, uses many aspects of the Christian as well as the Jewish faith, but in particularly Christian beliefs as foolish, hateful, bigoted and delusional. The truth is, King hates the true representation of the cross and his works, like those he idolized from his early childhood prove this.

When Stephen King, or anyone, enters into the realm of religion, they are treading on holy ground. To quote the Scriptures (which is the ultimate reality and truth); alongside science-fiction, nudity, cursing in God's name, sexual immorality, gore scenes, brutal violence on screen, and every other form of evil imaginable... it is evil. Proverb 6:16-19 proclaims that God hates a heart that deviseth evil imaginations. King's heart is a dark place of demonic fantasy, blasphemy against God, and loyalty to the demonic god of this world, Satan (2nd Corinthians 4:4).

Stephen King attacks Christianity much—blaspheming God, attacking the Bible, perverting the truth, tampering with things that he ought not. To say Stephen King is a Satan-worshipper, and demon-possessed would be mild to say the least. But if we look carefully at how he (King) operates, it is easy to see that King works well under the influence of demonic "guides". There are truths which hold to the idea which says that some individuals, given themselves over to the darkness, are used powerfully in the high order of the occult. It is this Author's opinion that, based on all of the evidence given, from King's early works, his deep, dark depression, his interest in forbidden subjects such as Witchcraft and the supernatural, that King is taking his cues from Satanic origins. This equally proves that his (Kings) aggressive overtones to true Christianity are a direct reflection of Satan's own feelings toward the church.

His (King) intense hatred for Bible-believing Christians is disturbing to say the least. Millions of people watch King's movies. Sinful men praise King for his works of darkness, calling him a "FRIGHTMASTER"; but in reality, King is a child of the Devil, promoting Satanism and hatred against the God of the Bible. Philippians 4:8, "Finally, brethren, whatsoever things are true, whatsoever things are honest, whatsoever things are just, whatsoever things are pure, whatsoever things are lovely, whatsoever things are of good report; if there be any virtue, and if there be any praise, think on these things."

To suggest that King's work is quality literary work, that King somehow is inspired by genuine love for humanity is far from the truth. When we peel away the layers, when we look behind the scope of King's work, we find a more deeper truth, a more sinister work, a work of hatred, anger and frustration, all toward a faith called Christianity and more importantly, toward the man called Jesus.

Anne Rice

Howard Allen Frances O'Brien was born October 4, 1941. Raised in New Orleans, Rice began, like so many others, a path into the occult. Raised in an observant Roman Catholic family, but became an atheist as a young adult. She began her professional writing career with the publication of Interview with the Vampire in 1976, while living in California, and began writing sequels to the novel in the 1980s. In the mid-2000s, following a publicized return to Catholicism, Rice published the novels Christ the Lord: Out of Egypt and Christ the Lord: The Road to Cana, fictionalized accounts of certain incidents in the life of Jesus. Several years later she distanced herself from organized Christianity, citing disagreement with the Churches stances on social issues but pledging that faith in God remained "central to [her] life."

Rice spent most of her childhood and teenage years in New Orleans, a city that forms the backdrop against which many of her works are set. Her early years were marked by coping with the family's poverty and her mother's alcoholism. She and her family lived in the rented home of her maternal grandmother, Alice Allen, known as "Mamma Allen," at 2301 St. Charles Avenue in the Irish Channel, which Rice says was widely considered a "Catholic Ghetto". Allen, who began working as a domestic shortly after separating from her alcoholic husband, was an important early influence in Rice's life, keeping the family and household together as Rice's mother sank deeper into alcoholism. Allen died in 1949, but the O'Briens remained in her home until 1956, when they moved to 2524 St. Charles Avenue, a former rectory, convent, and school owned by the parish, to be closer to both the church and support for Katherine's addiction. As a young child, Rice studied at St. Alphonsus School, a Catholic institution previously attended by her father.

On July 28, 2010, Rice publicly renounced her dedication to Christianity on her Face book page:
	"For those who care, and I understand if you don't: Today I quit being a Christian. I'm out. I remain committed to Christ as always but not to being "Christian" or to being part of Christianity. It's simply impossible for me to 'belong' to this quarrelsome, hostile, disputatious, and deservedly infamous group. For ten years, I've tried. I've failed. I'm an outsider. My conscience will allow nothing else."

Anne Rice and her associations with the occult, her attachments to spiritualism, mysticism and of course vampirism, is a reflection of something more deeper that we need to understand. There is a profound pattern of occultism associated with Rice which literally comes through every turn of the page. Anne Rice is unique in that she is not so much bold with the dark, supernatural occultist atmosphere which literally surrounds those like Stephen King or even Bram Stoker, yet, the one area in which Anne succeeds where others don't, is in the ability to seduce the reader into a world of Satan worship.

With the use of seductive characters like Lestat reflect a more subtle seduction to impressionable young people in today's society. They share the goal of living in harmony with nature, and they tend to view humanity's 'advancement' and separation from nature as the prime source of alienation. They see ritual as a tool to end that alienation and through the mists of the undead, young people are quickly seduced into a dark and overpowering world of lies and deceit, all created to destroy the young man or woman into Satan's lie.

Clearly, Rice has managed to influence horror films to such a degree that her works have secured several motion pictures, each dealing with the concept of vampirism, black magic, witchcraft and even human sacrifice, all in the name of literature. This makes Rice, whose own personal views of God and Christ, her failure to understand that Christ died for our sins, yet, by his own word, cannot accept or embrace that which is an abomination. Like every horror writer before her, Anne is yet one more disciple of the teachings of Satan's lie.

R. L. Stine

Robert Lawrence Stine was born on October 8th, 1943. A Columbus Ohio native, Stine later moved to New York where he would go on to develop and accomplish his dream as a horror writer for children. In 1986, Stine wrote his first horror novel, called Blind Date. He followed with many other novels, including The Babysitter, Beach House, Hit and Run, and The Girlfriend. He was also the co-creator and head writer for the Nickelodeon Network children's television show Eureka's Castle, original episodes of which aired as part of the Nick Jr. programming block during the 1989 to 1995 seasons.

The Stephen King of the pre-teen set, R.L. Stine is the wildly successful author of the Goosebumps books, a horror series for young readers. Stine began writing for young audiences early in his career, with work for Junior Scholastic Magazine and on books like 101 Silly Monster Jokes and Bozos on Patrol. He created and edited the comedy magazine Bananas before turning to teen horror with his 1986 novel Blind Date. Stine began the Fear Street series in 1989, and then launched the Goosebumps series in 1992. The Goosebumps books, with titles like Brain Juice, My Hairiest Adventure and It Came From Beneath the Sink!, were an international success and the series was turned into a syndicated TV series in 1995. Stine launched another series of stories, The Nightmare Room, in 1999; it also was adapted for television (in 2001). Like J.K. Rowling, Stine has been credited with encouraging young readers, while at the same time he has weathered criticism for writing stories based on the occult. His autobiography, It Came from Ohio! My Life as a Writer, was published in 1997.

If there ever was a writer who has done more, besides paving the way for J. K. Rowling's influence upon children with the occult, it is in fact R. L. Stine. Satan is a master of deception, and the one area in which he uses that same deception is through childlike innocence. Children have a clear innocence when they are young, their ability to understand or even "see" the supernatural is extremely high at this stage of their lives when they are 2 years old to about 11. it is during this time that, without spiritual, Godly direction is guided into the heart and mind of a child, the world, namely Satan's deception, will take over and begin to influence those same children into a forbidden world of occultist ideas and knowledge.

It is equally interesting to note that Nickelodeon, a network dedicate strictly to education as well as entertaining children as well as teens, merged R. L. Stine's work in "Goosebumps" and created a virtual series of TV. shows, books, and merchandise, all glorifying the occult with such topics as Witchcraft, the use of Mediums, Psychics, necromancy and the use of the Ouija board.

What Stephen King or Anne Rice did for adult horror, Stine has managed to do for introducing children into the occult. The Bible reminds us that under no circumstances are we ever to allow ourselves, or our children, to be associated, whether it be books, or cartoons or animation, affect our lives if it has to do with the occult and Satanic worship. God condemns such behavior, he compels us in his word not to allow anything which Satan uses to influence our spiritual being.

The strong connection between horror films and literary is a compelling one, components which reflect a deeper psychosis in relation to the occult, alcoholism, despair, and even death, are too big to ignore. The sad truth is, these men and women who have allowed themselves to become used, for whatever possible reason, whether it was fame, money, success, even love, Satan used to his advantage to bring about a greater deception, which was and still is, to seduce and then make comfortable the idea that he isn't real, that everything relating to demons and spirits and the occult is fantasy from the minds of troubled writers. That is the greater danger, to make it all suggest that it's not real, yet, at the same time, Satan uses these very same ingredients to manipulate the truth and draw men and women and especially young people, into a world of darkness which will ultimately bring bondage.

But there is a greater danger that we must take into account, and that is the use of literary which praises the occult, which glorifies the supernatural, that not only "conditions" the reader into accepting that which is evil, but it removes any built in resistance that the person might have to that which is clearly wrong. That is the greater danger, and the sooner we realize this and take the necessary steps to respond accordingly, nothing will ever change, books will still be written, movies will continue to be made and literally millions will be drawn into the dark world of the occult and seduce many into that very lie which was created not by the imagination of a man or woman, but by a fallen being, damned for all eternity in a future lake of fire, and his name is Satan.

Chapter Twelve
Vampire Lesbianism

During the post war era of WWI, the concept of the horror film was beginning to be birthed as the world itself was beginning to move past the war to end all wars. While most of the world began to rebuild, movie Studios and filmmakers were in the early development of the business of entertainment, and for some, the concept of horror seemed the time was right for a new form of fright.

In 1922, a new representation of vampire came onto the screen, that movie was none other than Nosferatu, the very first vampire movie. With that came the first on screen depiction of suggestive sexuality, but because society was still conservative in its approval of indecent imagery, movie makers had to be more clever in how they projected sex and sexuality. But by the time the 1930's had arrived, less than 10 years had past when Hollywood released its first major achievement - Dracula, and thus sexuality was born in the horror film.

With the arrival of sound, the scope and imagery of horror began to change. No longer did filmmakers have to rely on ghostly, dreamlike imagery to suspend people into an underworld of fanciful macabre, sound would actually make the world of horror come alive.

Even though the 1931 film Dracula contained the first imagery of sexuality, still, the makers of early horror films, much like most of the Hollywood productions coming out during this time, where still subjected to strict code of moral content. But that too was about to change.

For the next 40 years, the nation would slowly be coming out of a recession, a world war and the rebuilding of America. But trouble would once again be rattling the world through the conflicts of Korea and then Vietnam, the nation would again be tossed into a foreign conflict and face more changes at home, especially with the death of John Kennedy. The nation was changing and Hollywood began to take notice.

Horror films, by this time, had gone through many changes, but each change seemed to push the boundaries to reflect the current mood of the nation, but no change affected the genre more than the sexual revolution.

Social morality that had seen major growth within the nations culture was gone by the end of the decade as a huge rethink occurred in everything from hemlines to homosexuality. Horror movies, usually made for low budgets outside the mainstream studio system, offered the counterculture opportunities to debunk old taboos and explore new ways of perceiving sexual imagery.

Underground cinema dodged scrutiny, and therefore censorship. As well as being more open to nudity, on screen violence, and other tropes that challenged social morals, the drive-in teen audiences of the 1950s were growing up, and becoming wise to the empty promises of lurid titles and titillating posters, immune to the scare factor of rubber suits and miniaturized sets. They wanted horror that was more rooted in reality, more believable, more sophisticated, that dealt with some of the issues they faced in a rapidly changing world.

They, along with many, wanted sex and the sexual revolution gave filmmakers that opportunity to give what many within the population wanted. One aspect of sexuality that was taboo up until the late 60's was in fact lesbianism. Not even mainstream producers dared to resort to show sexual acts between two women, but with a new generation demanding change, producers were apt to find that avenue to both give them (the audience) what they desired as well as make money in the process.

By the time the 70's came along, horror films began to reflect the current mood of the generation, and what that generation wanted was progressive entertainment. This also included explicit sex. This paved the way how homosexuality could grip an entire generation in America, but it was helped along thru two avenues, a progressive movie studio in Britain and vampires.

Universal pictures had already established themselves as the family friendly studio when it came to their classic horror characters, although based on actual demonic gods and pagan origins, most families ignored, or where ignorant of the foundation of such ghouls as Dracula or The Mummy. But money troubles and a lack of interest from American audiences began to force Studios to rethink how they created content; enter Hammer Films.

In America, traditional moral standards were strong, even in film; the difficulty of movies to incorporate strong sexual content was still prohibited as the MPAA quickly tag any movie with an X rating. While America was finding its moral measuring stick, the UK, especially in Britain had already discovered its success of incorporating sexual content without fear of pressure from moral social groups, and Hammer Studios would find itself as the flagship of purveyors for sexual freedom.

Priding itself with its X-adult only content, Hammer Studios used soft core adult content within its revamped versions of the classic horror masterpieces from Dracula to Frankenstein. But it was Hammer's "Vampire Lovers" which started the slide into lesbianism, and when it crossed over the Atlantic, movie goers were quick to satisfy their lust and jumped onto Hammer's concept of soft porn vampirism.

The political mobilization of the gay & lesbian movements seen throughout much of the nation began to influence more of its culture, but still it had to break the barrier of its long objected stigma of immorality, the homosexual movement needed something, anything to bring it's movement to the forefront and horror seemed the perfect avenue.

Pornography during the 70's and 80's was making inward strides toward saturating the marketplace with adult films, and many of those within the industry who wanted a piece of the pie realized that by tapping into the soft porn erotica side of the business without truly becoming mixed into the likes of Larry Flynt or Hugh Hefner gave them the avenue to do it without being tagged a pornographer.

Since the lesbian vampire genre can allow nudity, blood, and sexual titillation in a "safe" fantasy structure, the industry standard of the mpaa would overlook much of what would normally be tagged an X rating and passed with a mere R rating. The fact is, the horror film, mainly the vampire erotica literally brought in the homosexual propaganda and captured the hearts of many, enticing them into the bondage of porn and sexual addiction. It was vampire films under the guise of Gothic entertainment and one English studio which literally transformed an entire movement to begin its indoctrination of lesbianism into our culture.

Chapter Thirteen
The Halloween Connection

It would be impossible for me to do a book on the history, the influence and the dangers of horror films without dealing with what most would conceive as one of the biggest connections to the horror movie. To better understand the role Horror films have played upon our society, we must first look at the one holiday horror films thrives on - Halloween.

The word Halloween was first used in the 16th century and represents a Scottish variant of the fuller All-Hallows'-Even ("evening"), that is, the night before All Hallows' Day.

The Halloween holiday is commonly thought to have pagan roots, even though the etymology of the word is Christian. Historian Nicholas Rogers, exploring the origins of Halloween, notes that while "some folklorists have detected its origins in the Roman feast of Pomona, the goddess of fruits and seeds, or in the festival of the dead called Parentalia, it is more typically linked to the Celtic festival of Samhain, derived from the Old Irish Samuin meaning "summer's end".

Samhain was the first and the most important of the four quarter days in the medieval Irish and Scottish calendar and, falling on the last day of autumn, it was a time for stock-taking and preparation for the cold winter months ahead. There was also a sense that this was the time of year when the physical and supernatural worlds were closest and magical things could happen.

The souls of the dead were supposed to revisit their homes on Samhain eve. To ward off these spirits, the Gaels built huge, symbolically regenerative bonfires and invoked the help of the gods through animal and perhaps even human sacrifice. In the Western Isles of Scotland the Sluagh, or fairy host was regarded as composed of the souls of the dead flying through the air, and the feast of the dead at Halloween was likewise the festival of the fairies.

October 31 is the most important day in the satanic year. [It is known as the devil's birthday.] It marks the Celtic new year. It was the end of the growing season. It became a festival of death. On this day, the god of the Celtics was to have called up the spirits of the wicked dead who had died during the past year. At the same time, other evil spirits arose and went about the countryside harassing the people. On October 31, the Celtics expected to be harassed by ghosts, evil spirits and demons; and it was no fun and games to them. They would light bonfires to guide the spirits to their own town and to ward off evil spirits.

Druids

The Celtics had priests called druids. On October 31, the druids went from house to house demanding certain foods, and all those who refused were cursed. The people were tormented by means of magic. As they went, the druids carried large turnips which they had hollowed out and on which they had carved demon faces as charms. Each one was believed to contain the demon spirit that personally led or guided that priest: his little god.

Divination

Those who practiced fortune telling and divination found that this was the night that they had the most success. They called upon Satan to bless their efforts. One form of divination was to put apples in a tub and bob for them. The one who first successfully came up with one without putting them in his teeth was to have good luck throughout the year. They would then peel the apples and throw the peeling over their shoulders and then quickly look around. They expected to see a vision or an apparition of the one they were to marry.

Sacrifices

These things happened several centuries before CHRIST. Sacrifices were made to the gods, especially the god of death - Samhain (pronounced Sah win). Sacrifices all the way from vegetable to human were offered. This went on and on, and, in some parts of the world, still goes on today.

8th Century

In the 8th century, the Pope, in an effort to get the people to quit the festival of Sam hain, invented All Saints Day (Nov. 1). This was an attempt to get the people to turn away from the horrible observance of Sam hain. All Saints Day was intended to honor the martyrs of the Roman persecutions. It did not work! It never works to Christianize a pagan holiday. The holy and the profane do not mix.

The Middle Ages

In the Middle Ages, there was a great revival of satanic practices and witchcraft and magic - like there is today. During this time the belief developed that witches traveled on broomsticks to the black Sabbaths to worship Satan on October 31. They were guided by spirits in the form of black cats. The Druids worshiped cats believing them to be reincarnated evil people.

The Heroes of Halloween

When we look at the spell or the roots of Halloween and how it casts its spirit upon our world, the true nature, the prophet, the "preacher" of this Satanic holiday which trumpets its message of occultism is in fact the horror film.

There are rudiments or stages; levels, if you will, which promote and celebrate this specific holiday and in turn, the very holiday gives the horror film its much needed light in which to operate. Take for example one aspect of Halloween - the Witch.

The Witch

In an Illustrated History of Witchcraft, by Peter Haining. He states, "The witch is, without doubt, one of the most enduring figures in superstition and literature. Whether portrayed as an aged crone astride a broomstick off on some mission of evil, or else a young girl dancing naked with her companions in a wooded grove, she can be found in carvings of antiquity or the columns of today's newspapers...since the Middle Ages, (writings have) shown her as an enemy of humanity, a solitary being able to compact with the Devil to work all manner of supernatural powers."

The first famous witch in history is the Witch of Endor. I Samuel 28 relate how King Saul went to her in an effort to get in touch with the dead prophet of God, Samuel. He needed advice on how to defeat the Philistines. He should have known better because Exodus 22:18 prescribed being a witch as a capital crime, punishable by death. Again Deuteronomy 18:9-14 warned that God's children were to have nothing to do with the OCCULT. Even in the New Testament (Revelation 21:8 Galatians 5:20 KJV) lists the practitioners of witchcraft as being excluded from God's kingdom.

Though witches like to make a distinction between themselves and Satanist's, there really is no distinction biblically speaking. They might play little word games masking the connection between Lucifer and Satan but the power behind Satanism and Witchcraft is the same-Satan, (formerly called Lucifer before his rebellion against God) and his demonic hordes.

When the Bible makes reference to witchcraft it means anyone who is involved in some form of the occult. The word occult comes from the Latin meaning secret, hidden, or esoteric (private; understood only by a few) knowledge or practices.

The Wizard (Warlock)

When we begin to examine the occult, the offices within the occult structure, we see there are different positions, levels or offices of authority in the occult pyramid, and the one which garners favoritism among many, especially children because of a certain boy wizard, is the Warlock.

Because of the huge popularity brought about by Harry Potter (which we will look at more closely in the next chapter), many children, and even some adults, have become fascinated by the concept of a Wizard. But what exactly is a Wizard?

A Wizard is a magician, which may also be known in various regions as a magic-user, mage, magister, archmage, sorcerer/sorceress, shugenja, witch, wizard, warlock, wu jen, enchanter/enchantress, illusionist, diviner, conjurer, or thaumaturge; depending on the broad contextual range of occult practices or cultural beliefs, is someone who uses or practices magic that derives from supernatural or occult sources.

Wizards have become popular in our culture, whether in film or in literary, the wizard has influenced many in its occult snare, including children. Who can forget the odd looking old fellow behind the dreaded curtain in the 1939 children's film classic, "The Wizard of Oz"? The film, a cinema classic to this day, is regularly seen and viewed by children of all ages and across the globe. Yet, it is in fact the "Wizard of Oz" which has managed to ensnare many without even knowing they have been lured into the dark world of the occult. That in itself, is the power of the occult and the power of Satan's lie.

A brief mention of Oz

When L. Frank Baum wrote, "The Wizard of Oz", he did so under great authority on the occult. Baum, himself a member of the Theosophical Society, which is an organization based on occult research and the comparative study of religions. Baum had a deep understanding of Theosophy and, consciously or not, created an allegory of Theosophical teachings when he wrote the Wizard of Oz.

The Theosophical Society was an occult organization, mainly based on the teachings of Helena P. Blavatsky, which seeks to extract the common roots of all religions in order to form a universal doctrine.

Before writing the Wizard of Oz, Baum wrote a series of articles introducing readers to Theosophy, including his personal views on Buddha, Mohammed, Confucius and Christ. At that time, he wasn't a member of the Theosophical Society but he already showed a deep understanding of its philosophy.

Two years after writing those articles, L. Frank Baum and his wife Maud Gage joined the Theosophical Society in Chicago. The archives of the Theosophical Society in Pasadena, California recorded the start of their membership as September 4th, 1892. In 1890, the Wizard of Oz was published. When asked about how Baum got his inspiration for the story, he replied:

"It was pure inspiration…It came to me right out of the blue. I think that sometimes the Great Author has a message to get across and He has to use the instrument at hand. I happened to be that medium, and I believe the magic key was given me to open the doors to sympathy and understanding, joy, peace and happiness."-- L. Frank Baum

Two things which should stand out to the reader, 1) Baum openly admits that he became a Medium which allowed a spirit to come into him to create (by mere inspiration he claims) Oz and 2) he (Baum) was given a Magic key to open up a world of fantasy, which has lead many into a world of the occult.

Baum suggests that it was his imagination that helped him create his literary classic, yet, he readily admits to being a medium, a conduit to the spirit world, which he gained precise information by way of occultist methods thru his friend, Blavatsky. When a person opens up the doorway into the spirit world through the means of the occult, as Baum had done like so many others before him, going all the way back to the witch of Endor, that individual becomes a pawn for a greater deception, in that he or she becomes used by the power of Satan for his bidding. In the case of the Witch of Endor, it was forbidden knowledge. In the case of Baum, it was inspiration to create a literary piece that not only has stood the test of time to this day, it has remained one of *the* classic films for children and adults worldwide.

I contend that the Wizard of Oz was not only a demonic inspiration, it was a master plan designed and schemed by Satan himself to bring about a deception which would last for generations. Like Harry Potter in our current day, The Wizard of Oz has outlasted and outpaced many great classic literary novels of its day (1890) all the way into the 21st century. No other novel to this day, except for maybe the Harry Potter series, can claim that title of lasting throughout the years. This is not due to the literary prowess of Baum, but more to the power of Satanic influence. When Satan begins a work, he will continue that work until it's fully utilized. I believe this is why Harry Potter became such a huge success in this decade, there was a fullness of time for the next arrival of Satan's lie upon a new generation due to the waning impact of the Oz upon children and the changing times. Satan is no fool when it comes to the changing nature of men, he is always two steps ahead.

The Wizard of Oz's great success is a testament not toward Baum's ability to create a timeless classic epic of storytelling and fantasy, it was a testament of Satan's ability to impose a lie upon men to create a legacy of deceit. Written during the 1890's, when most of the country was Christians, Baum's story anticipated the people's abandonment of traditional religions in the coming future and the embrace of a new form of spirituality. This paved the way for Harry Potter.

Werewolves

A werewolf, also known as a lycanthrope, is a mythological or folkloric human with the ability to shape shift into a wolf or an anthropomorphic wolf-like creature, either purposely or after being placed under a curse and/or lycanthropic affliction via a bite or scratch from a werewolf, or some other means. This transformation is often associated with the appearance of the full moon.

Almost everyone can remember the 1941 horror film - "The Wolf Man" starring Lon Chaney Jr., it was that particular movie by Universal, which literally launched the ancient concept of werewolves in the general public. From that time to present, werewolves have become a fixture in our daily lives, from movies to television series, it's almost as if werewolves popped up out of nowhere. Yet a better understanding of this goes further back than 1941.

During middle ages, especially from 15th to 17th century, Europe was under the dark shadow of ignorance and superstitions. Towns were underdeveloped and people lived near woods. The fear of wolves was like a nightmare. Their attacks were so frequent and atrocious in nature that people even feared to travel from one place to another. Every morning, countryside people would find half-eaten human limbs scattered on their fields.

The first recorded Werewolf sighting took place around the countryside of German town Cologne and Bedburg in 1591. An age-old pamphlet describes those shivering moments vividly. Few people cornered a large wolf and set their dogs upon it. They started to pierce it with sharp sticks and spears. Surprisingly the ferocious wolf did not run away or tried to protect itself, rather it stood up and turned out to be a middle-aged man he was Peter Stubbe from the same village.

Stubbe was put on a torture wheel where he confessed sixteen murders including two pregnant women and thirteen children. The history behind his downfall was rather bizarre. He had started to practice sorcery when he was only 12 and was so obsessed with it that even tried to make a pact with the Devil. Wearing a magic girdle he started to attack his enemies, real or imaginary.

After several months, he would take the guise of a wolf and continued with his evil acts with more brutality. In the wolf form he used to tear up victims' throats and suck warm blood from veins. Gradually his thirst for blood grew and he roamed around fields in search of prey.

The savagery of his crimes was beyond imagination. The trial record motioned few of them. Once two men and a woman were walking along a road that went through the forest Stubbe used to hide in. He called one of them into the forest. When the man did not return for a long time the second one followed his trail and also disappeared into the forest. When both the man didn't return for a long time the woman ran for her life. Later, two mangled male corpses were recovered from the forest, but the woman's body never reappeared. It was believed that Stubbe had devoured it all. Young girls playing together or milking the cows in the fields were his frequent victims. He used to chase them like a hound, catch the slowest one, rape and kill her. Then he would drink hot blood and eat tender flesh from her body. However; the most gruesome sin he committed was upon his own son. He took him to a nearby forest, cracked the poor child's skull open and ate brain from it.

No punishment could match the magnitude of Stubbe's crime. His flesh was pulled off with red-hot pincer, his arms and legs were broken and he was finally decapitated. His carcass was burned to ashes.

The Magistrate of Bedburg built a grim monument remembering the ghastly incident. Workmen put the torture wheel atop a tall pole with Stubbe's head above it structured with the likeliness of a wolf. Sixteen pieces of yard long wood cuts were hung from the rim of the wheel commemorating poor souls of the victims. The words of Stubbe's trial and execution spread across the lands in no time. His brutality, atrocity and savagery were beyond human comprehension and were readily related with the behavior of a wolf. People started to believe that such individuals with the shadow of wolves were living among them. They named them Werewolves.

Werewolves are a direct connection to Witchcraft and the occult. Although not real, the werewolf is a representation of evil, it takes the idea of man changing into a beast which in of itself distorts the word of God, for God, when he created man, made man perfect and good. There was nothing evil about the first man until his initial disobedience in the garden.

What we see taking place with the concept and glorification of werewolves is the acceptance of something God prohibits among his people. Whenever we see seduction on this level, it's to deceive many into a dark world of the occult and why werewolves are yet one more aspect of the Halloween connection to horror films.

Vampires

Nothing suggests occultism like vampires. From the 16th to the 18th centuries, belief in vampires seems to have been especially prevalent in areas of Eastern Europe such as Serbia, Russia and Romania - home to Transylvania which Stoker immortalized as 'vampire country'. The word 'vampyr' seems to have arrived in the English language from Serbian via German, and is similar to the Serbo-Croat word for witch.

Folklore in the region said that vampires were corpses who rose from the dead and terrorized their living neighbors. It was eastern European folklore that gave us the idea that garlic is a protection against vampires (Stoker used this idea in Dracula), and the traditions of how to kill a vampire such as beheading and nailing a wooden stake through the heart.

Belief in vampires was so fervent at this time that corpses were sometimes ordered to be dug up so that they could have a stake put through their heart and / or their head cut off. Garlic was often shoved up the nose of a corpse before burial to prevent them returning as a vampire. When the corpses were dug up it was noted that some had rosy cheeks and blood red lips - this may have given rise to the belief that these 'undead' were drinking the blood of the living.

Vlad the Impaler (son of Vlad Dracula) was a real historical figure famed for his cruelty - his practice of impaling his enemies on wooden stakes to die a slow death - and also his military prowess with which he defeated the Ottoman Turks. Vlad the Impaler ruled his subjects with an iron fist and is remembered as both a fearful overlord and a national hero who defended against Turkish invasion.

The idea of the historical Vlad the Impaler (Vlad Tepes in Romanian) as a real vampire is expertly explored in the novel ' The Historian' by Elizabeth Kostova. However, the real history books have no record as Vlad the Impaler as a vampire - the association is entirely down to Bram Stoker choosing the name 'Dracula' for his vampire villain.

This should be very important to the reader, Vlad Dracula was a man full of great evil, this we know thru ancient records. Vlad would impale his enemies, even those within his own kingdom to stakes, no one was spared from his wrath and evil - even children were subject to his hatred and venom.

What normal parent who loves their children would allow their child to not only dress up as a vampire, but embrace something so cold, so wicked, and so cruel as one such as Vlad Dracula?

There are three categories of the Occult...

1. Divination -- Seeking to know the past, present or future by astrology; horoscopes; channeling; tarot; etc. This can include animal or human sacrifice.

2. Sorcery or Magic(k) -- Seeking to control or manipulate reality for ones own purposes. This can include animal or human sacrifice to accomplish that end.

3. Spiritism -- Seeking to communicate with the dead or other entities through a medium.

Generally speaking, it is accurate to say that those who practice witchcraft hold the following four beliefs.

Animism -- The belief that all objects (rocks, trees, wind, plants, mountains etc.) is alive and has a soul.

Pantheism -- The belief that everything is divine (god). Divinity is inseparable from and immanent in everything such as nature and humanity. In fact we are divine or gods.

Polytheism -- Belief in many deities (gods). They also believe in multi-levels of reality.

What do those in Wicca do?

1. DABBLERS -- They are experimenting or playing around with the occult.

2. ECLECTIC or SELF-STYLED OCCULTISTS -- They have moved from the dabbling stage into deeper involvement. They are developing their own individualized occultist religion and developing personalized beliefs and practices.

3. RELIGIOUS OCCULTIST -- These people openly belong to an official occult group. Their group is often tax exempt and is protected by the first amendment. They deny involvement in any criminal activity and seek to present their beliefs as a legitimate religion. Lori Cabot (official witch of Salem, Mass.) heads the Temple of Isis. There is the Church of Circle Wicca; The Witches International Craft Association and numerous others.

4. INTRA-GENERATIONAL OCCULTIST -- These are clandestine (secret), family religions that pass their occultist practices from one generation to another. This category of occultists seems to be well organized, very secretive and is often very dangerous.

For the most part, wherever you find witchcraft you will likely find nudity because many of their rituals are performed "Skyclad" (in the nude). Witches practice divination, which is the attempt to obtain information regarding the past, present or future through occultist methods like astrology, channeling (inviting a spirit to possess your body), tarot cards, crystal balls, etc.

Magic is a cornerstone of witchcraft. When I speak of magic I am not talking about "slight-of-hand." I am talking about invoking or attempting to invoke an invisible force (demons) for use in influencing, manipulating, or controlling a given situation to accomplish ones own will in a situation.

Then there is the common practice among witches and occult followers of "drawing down the moon." The high priestess of the coven usually stands "Skyclad" with arms outstretched to the sky and calls down the goddess or invites the goddess to possess them. In response, the high priestess will often enter a trance state and become the voice of the goddess. During this time she functions as the goddess incarnate (goddess in the flesh) within the magic circle. Whatever she says is supposedly directly from the goddess.

Witches and coven members practice many immoral and perverted sexual practices as a part of their rituals. These rituals are often accompanied by alcohol and drug use.

It is obvious that God does not want his children to have anything to do with witches or witchcraft. I believe we should "Abstain from all appearance of evil." (I Thessalonians 5:22) Certainly that would include dressing like a witch, wizard or sorcerer.

In almost every aspect of Halloween, the Witch can be directly traced from its occult/pagan/Satanic web of deceit to the glorification found in many horror films made today as well as those in the past. Halloween is harmful because of its emphasis on violence and death.

Halloween emphasizes thru Horror films Fear

An article in the Milwaukee Journal, entitled "Haunted House Fun: It could become a nightmare for kids" stated, "It's just for fun, you know that. But to a young child, a trip through a `haunted house' created for Halloween could be a nightmare." Psychologist Marvin Berkowitz of Marquette University said, "Some haunted houses can frighten an adult." He warned that a child must "go in with the right mental set." He said, "Make sure they know it's going to be a fun scare, not a real scare." The article went on to day that even though you do your best to let the child know this he can be traumatized by such an experience."

God never gives us the spirit of fear, but of love, joy and a peaceful, or sound mind.

Halloween emphasizes the Occult through the worship of Horror Films

John Carpenter, Stephen King, Anne Rice, Tim Burton and Bram Stoker, they all have one thing in common - they celebrate the spirit of Halloween in each of their works. Halloween, the horror film, the occult spirit which overlays one another, do so because they each are dedicated to spreading Satanic propaganda.

Halloween is the tie that binds when it comes to horror films, they are literally one unit and because of their unique nature, they both, the horror movie and Halloween, serve a purpose, to preach the message of occultism. Without Halloween, the horror film could continue in its agenda and still, on some level, reach many with its message of violence and spiritualism, without horror films, Halloween could continue, on some level, continue along its path of promoting the dark arts, it's cultic secrets and ancient pagan ways, but its impact upon society would be severely limited simply because the horror film utilizes visual means to bring its message for all to see and visualization is a powerful medium unlike Halloween, which uses history through the written text to bring its message to life. This makes the horror film more needed and more desirable for the enemy to utilize along with the roots of Halloween. Either way, it's a deadly cocktail for all who drink it.

Chapter Fourteen

Slasher Films

In our ever changing society, things do indeed take a turn into different directions and over time, change to conform to our changing culture. One in particular is how horror films are changing to a more violent tendency and senseless violence in the content of their storylines. It seems as though the monster truly has been unleashed.

The truest definition of what is termed as a "slasher" film typically involves a mysterious psychopathic killer stalking and killing a sequence of victims usually in a graphically violent manner, often with a cutting tool such as a knife or axe. Although the term "slasher" may be used as a generic term for any horror movie involving graphic acts of murder, the slasher as a genre has its own set of characteristics which set it apart from related genres like the splatter film.

Possibly the earliest slasher-type film is Thirteen Women (1932), which tells the story of an old college sorority whose former members are set against one another by a vengeful peer, seeking penance for the prejudice they bestowed on her because of her mixed race heritage. Another film influential to the subgenre is Michael Powell's Peeping Tom (1960). The film's plot centers around a man who kills women while using a portable movie camera to record their dying expressions.

The film was immensely controversial when first released; critics called it misogynistic (as would critics condemn the slasher films during its golden age). Alfred Hitchcock's Psycho (1960), released three months after Peeping Tom, and is often seen as an important forerunner to the genre. Even though the villain's body count is only two, the film's "whodunit" plot structure, knife-wielding and mentally disturbed killer, twist ending and 'stalking' camera technique proved influential on films to come. Another early pioneer of the subgenre is director Francis Ford Coppola's controversial 1963 film, "Dementia 13", which was rushed into production following Psycho's success at the box office.

The 1970s were arguably the Golden Age for exploitation films, films which tended to be low budget affairs specializing in suggestive or explicit sex, sensational violence, drug use, nudity, freaks, gore, the bizarre, destruction, rebellion and/or mayhem. While such films have existed since the earliest days of moviemaking, they were popularized in the 1960s with the general relaxing of cinematic taboos in the United States and Europe. Additionally, low budget filmmakers used sensational elements to attract audiences away from television.[citation needed] Slasher films are often considered exploitation films because of their use of their often low budgets, nudity, gore and shock techniques. Arguably the most controversial of all exploitation films was Wes Craven's The Last House on the Left (1972). The film was produced by Sean S. Cunningham, who later went on to direct the popular Friday the 13th.

Particularly important to the development of the slasher subgenre was Tobe Hooper's 1974 film The Texas Chain Saw Massacre, which featured a mysterious masked killer known as Leather face, building on the slasher villain formula.

One thing that separates slashers from thrillers and murder mysteries is the level of violence. Slashers shift the focus of the film from such trivialities as "plot" and "character development" and instead concentrate on the killing. Storylines are basically constructed around giving the killer reason and opportunity to do what he does best: murder and mayhem. The deaths are violent and graphic, and the more originality shown in the methods and tools used, the better.

The success of slasher films are equal to the number of people who are willing to go and pay money to either sit in a theater along with others, buy the DVD or rent for the evening. The simple truth is, people not only like the violence and mayhem they are viewing, they love it as well. Is there a deeper connection to slasher films and our current culture? It seems so.

Our nation seems to relish gore and violence. It glorifies murder and sadistic or even ritualistic killings and for a society which has seen thousands of hours of television violence, violent news reports, violence overseas and violence in our music we listen to, it pays to reason that slasher films are simply giving what the people desire, what they want.

John Carpenter's Halloween (1978) is often considered to be the first "true" slasher in terms of tying all of these components together, thus setting the standard by which all other films are judged. Throughout the 80's and into the mid 90's, slasher films began to decrease in numbers as well as audience approval. But then, sometime in early 2002, a heavy metal rock musician who prided himself in sadistic and overtly Satanic symbolism in his music and road act, Rob Zombie started to venture into the horror film business, but with a different angle, taking a direct cue from his onstage persona, Zombie began to mix his heavy metal Goth music with horror films and a re-birth was born.

 Robert Bartleh Cummings (Rob Zombie) has opened the door to horror by incorporating both its occult roots (Cummings not only desired to follow a more occult path as his predecessors, he had his name legally changed to Rob Zombie in 1996). With his own personal studies of the occult, (an interest he particularly found appealing) Zombie has seemed to tap into a style of movie making that appears to be finding a larger audience with each film he directs and releases. This is yet once again, a direct relation to the occult and it's early beginnings.

Crowley's impact on Zombies work as a horror director is quite clear in his films, in one particular film, reproductions of Aleister Crowley's paintings of demonic figures can be seen in his House of a 1000 corpses. In another scene, a tape player is also sent down and it keeps repeating a slowed down version of Aleister Crowley's poem "The Poet", read by himself (found on a CD called The Great Beast Speaks which is the only known recording of Crowley). The line from the poem that gets repeated over and over is: "Bury me in a nameless grave".

Zombie's tribute to the past Satanist is made clear. Yet, many people, especially young people have no understanding what is taking place or going on, nor would they care. Still, Satan's scheme remains the same, to kill, steal and destroy. Under no circumstances should we as believers, or even those who do not know Christ themselves, allow themselves to listen to or watch images, films or books which promote an evil such as Satanism. For it is Satanism which has caused so many to fall into a world of despair and the only answer to that is the saving grace of Jesus Christ.

Whatever plans men like Carpenter, King or even Zombie might have planned as their next haunting, violent film, knowledge is power, and when we have that knowledge, then that power Satan would attempt to deceive as well as destroy many with it, becomes hindered by the truth. God gives us truth found in his word and Satan, once he and his tactics are exposed, are no match for that truth, or that light, for that light is Jesus Christ himself, to which no one can stand up against. For men like King or Zombie will one day bow before the King of Kings and the Lord of Lords and on that day, when they stand before the Savior of the world, they will have only themselves to answer for and they too, along with their devilish master, will proclaim Jesus Christ Lord.

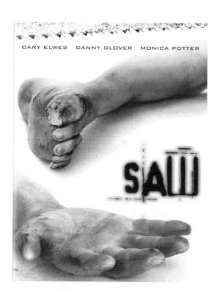

Chapter Fifteen
The Harry Potter Affect

"Woe to those who call evil good, and good evil..." Isaiah 5:20

When it comes to the power of influence the occult, whether it be Witchcraft or paganism or black magic, there is one segment of horror films which has had a profound influence upon a culture, a generation of young people that has not only enlightened them to the world of the occult, but it has virtually conditioned them to be lured into a more darker world of mature occultist ideas and behavior and that is thru a small boy wizard named Harry Potter.

Now, some would say, "I don't see the connection between Harry Potter and horror films" and on the outside this would be true - on the outside. But if we actually take the time to peer into this vast domain created by J. K. Rowling, we will begin to see something more devious taking place, then and only then will we begin to see the real truth, the primer which literally connects the dots from rudimentary occult symbolism to full blown Satanic rituals caught on screen and hidden deep into the pages of her books.

It is easy to forget, surrounded by contemporary Western society, that only a few generations ago talk of witchcraft and the like was heresy, a crime for which many millions of people were slaughtered, tortured, burned alive or drowned by the authority of the Church. The success of the Potter phenomenon heralds a new era in which the old religious order is powerless, and the world is governed by a secular new order - Novus Ordo Seclorum.

So how does this relate to horror films? It relates because Harry Potter is the full representation of deception, it relates because Harry Potter, like the Twilight movies, like the current trend of Disney, candy coated animations such as Franken Weenie are symbolisms of ancient pagan occultist views and religion. It relates because Satan has cleverly schemed the ability to deceive through vague storylines which condition children into the occult, which nurtures them into a forbidden world of darkness and evil. Harry Potter is the symbolism of creating something new and appealing to the masses which then enable people to lower their guard against the Satanic deception it brings. That is the direct relation Harry Potter has toward horror films.

When Rowling's fifth Potter book, The Order of the Phoenix, came out, it came out in a rather strange and symbolist way. The book, contains 666 pages excluding the prologue, and it first went on sale in a series of unusual opening ceremonies held in major book shops throughout the world at exactly midnight on the eve of the Summer Solstice. In Druid and ancient occult practices, this is a direct symbolism to pagan practices. Yet thousands of children and young adults stood in line waiting for their chance to buy and read the latest of a boy wizard and his quest to defeat the evil Warlock, Voldemort.

Harry Potter *is* a new version horror film but packaged differently than most traditional, mainline horror films which appeal to older, mature young people and adults. Like the early cartoons which came out during the late 60's throughout the 1980's, Harry Potter was cleverly packaged to appeal to a wider, and younger audiences. Yet the components remained the same.

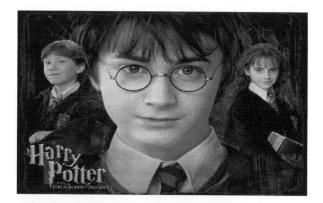

As in Old Testament days, today's world sees God's guidelines concerning occult influences as a hindrance to their quest for mystical thrills. In contrast, blending good and evil makes sense to postmodern churches. And as Harry and his friend Hermione point out, such compromise serves the pluralistic vision for "common good."

John Granger, author of "Looking for God in Harry Potter", may be the most effective promoter of this dialectical heresy. He puts the entire series into an occult context. Notice the references to the union of opposites -- and to the occult use of Scriptures -- in Granger's quotes:

"...the principal activity of alchemy is the chemical marriage of the imbalanced 'arguing couple': masculine sulfur and feminine quicksilver. These two qualities have to be reconciled and resolved (die and be reborn) before then can be rejoined in a perfected golden unity. Opposites have to be reconciled and resolved for there to be a new life.

"Alchemists frequently cited Christ's words: '...except a corn of wheat fall into the ground and die, it abideth alone: but if it die, it bringeth forth much fruit.' (John 12:24)."[3, page 44]

Those who immerse their minds in Rowling's occult message enter into a virtual experience -- not of Christian redemption -- but of this magical merger of good and evil. God warns us to shun any such "common ground" between His Truth and the world's illusions. For,

"...what fellowship has righteousness with lawlessness? And what communion has light with darkness? And what accord has Christ with Belial? Or what part has a believer with an unbeliever? And what agreement has the temple of God with idols? For you are the temple of the living God. As God has said: 'I will dwell in them and walk among them.... Therefore 'Come out from among them and be separate.'" 2 Corinthians 6:14-17

Rowling's occultist idea compromises the truth and corrupts the mind. It pleases man, not God. This makes Harry Potter a seductive tool in bridging the gap between horror films, the occult and children. Once you have managed to seduce the children, then nothing is impossible from that point forward.

J.K. Rowling, like her predecessors before her, such as Crowley, Stoker and Poe, came from insignificance to prominence in just a short matter of time. Like Poe or even Baum, Rowling was a struggling single mother of two, living in a time of economic downturn and literally only seeing her life dwindle away as she survived as so many before her through the welfare system. Then came Harry.

As I have said before, there are spaces of time in which Satan will search for that right person, the right time and the right message to fit into his greater plan, Rowling fit into all three. Within five short years, from literally poverty to prosperity far beyond anyone's possible dream, J.K. Rowling swiftly by-passed every obstacle along the way to literary riches. Not even Stephen King or Anne Rice can say the same! What took King or Rice or even Bram Stoker several hard, lean years to achieve their success in their field, and even then only saw regional royalties, it only took Rowling a couple of years, and unlike her literary friends, managed to secure more than 1 billion in overall personal earnings from Harry Potter series as well as the movie rights and merchandising. Rowling has out paced and out earned Stephen King, Anne Rice, Tom Clancy and Danielle Steel, put together.

So what makes Rowling unique? An anointing.

There is such a thing called a "dark anointing". This is where someone has purposefully allowed themselves to be taken over by a spirit of deception to bring about a message for the general public. Rowling came at a time when horror films and strong visual horror books were limited to older teens and adults. The years of dabbling with the occult was being tested by many in the entertainment industry, but still, the influence of the occult, whether it be Witchcraft, fortune telling or even black magic, was still, at best, random and remote with little major influence to bring about mass appeal.

Satan, like our heavenly Father, has his own spiritual children. Jesus proved this in John 8:44, when he said, "Your are of your Father, the Devil!" What Christ was saying is clear, when we reject the cross, when we turn blindly from the truth, his light cannot pierce the sin filled soul of man because man would rather be a willful sinner than a saved creation God originally designed him to be. This is the power of the cross, yet, Satan, like he has done all throughout modern and ancient civilizations, hand selected certain individuals to success, giving them talent, political power or great wealth, in exchange for their allegiance.

There is no doubt, with Rowling's sudden rise in popularity, wealth and influence among millions of children with her books on witchcraft and the occult, she, like Baum and like Stoker, filled a void between the occult and childhood innocence. This makes Rowling suspect in her works as well as in her sudden rise to fame and exposure. Yes, there will always be critics who will say that it was only hard work and a natural talent that brought Rowling her desired success, but is that true? The truth is, no, it's not.

Rowling herself admits to a certain degree of her belief in the occult, ""It's important to remember that we all have magic inside us." But whether or not Rowling was influenced by the occult, and many indications suggest she indeed was, it's important to understand that her acceptance and belief in the supernatural, her inquiries into pagan circles, covens and Wicca, all indicate an individual desiring to open herself to the dark forces which rule the current world system as we know it.

What Harry Potter accomplished in its vast 10 years of success, was condition a generation of young people into a world of witches, vampires, demons and Satanic ritual. Harry Potter is the link which brought children into a larger world of the masters of horror, ripe for picking and the only outcome was a generation lost to the world of the occult. Is it no great wonder that when the first Potter film debuted, occult stores literally ran out of books concerning witchcraft, Satanism, black magic. Even owls became victims of this sudden interest in occult nature of animals. Some stores even prohibited children from buying certain animals featured in any of the 7 films of Harry Potter. Satan did more with a boy wizard than Stoker did with a vampire, and the people decided it so.

Chapter Sixteen
A Christian Response to evil

How should we respond to horror films as believers in Christ? The genre has undeniable pagan roots and worse, deep Satanic origins. Should we avoid it completely? Should we watch, rent or buy popular horror movies that glorify sex, nudity, occult symbolism? Or, should we seek to engage in it fully in order to see people come to Christ? Ultimately, our decision must be informed by Scripture and by a desire to see God glorified.

To attempt to discuss and deal with any believer's connection with horror films or even books relating to the horror genre, we need to establish a few things. The first thing we need to understand is, horror films are undeniably rooted in the occult, there is no argument otherwise. Second, no Christian who truly desires to live right and conform to the image of Christ can, or would place themselves in the midst of such present darkness.

Christians should understand that horror films and all that it brings to the imagination–death imagery, superstition, expressions of debauched revelry– are fundamentally opposed to the gospel of Jesus Christ. God has given everyone a conscience that responds to His truth (Romans 2:14-16), and the conscience is the Christian's ally in the evangelistic enterprise. Christians should take time to inform the consciences of friends and family with biblical truth regarding God, the Bible, sin, Christ, future judgment, and the hope of eternal life in Jesus Christ for the repentant sinner.

As stated above, the horror genre is completely incompatible with the Christian faith. That said, what we are called to do when it comes to the horror genre, not to mention the bi-products from horror such as books, television programs and comics, is to shine the light on a well planned, well implemented program designed and orchestrated by Satan himself.

Stories that involve ghosts, demons, gore, sexual immorality and occultism draw our minds away from the things we should be dwelling upon. These are the things that are designed by their very nature to hinder the believer into a world of deception. For the believer to become apart of those things which God strictly warns us in the word not to partake of, is not meant to deprive us from something that the world considers "fun", it's to relay a very important message, and that message is, "Don't corrupt yourselves with evil!"

While it's true that we are *in* the world, we are not *of* this world. When a person becomes a born again in Christ, they have changed their citizenship from this present world to God's eternal home, our priorities change, our ideas change, and our belief system changes to reflect more of a God centered truth found in the word. That is aspect of us as believers. This makes anything associated with the things of this world, or worse, of Satan, incompatible with our Christian walk. That's why God desires us to avoid such evil, not because he doesn't want us to enjoy entertainment, but because he understands more than us the real power, the real agenda of the evil one.

Satan, the word says, seeks to kill, steal and destroy. It is Satan himself who has desired to destroy the lives of both the saved and unsaved and he does so through many means and devices, to some he uses sex, while others he uses wealth and power, for others it could mean a simple better paying job. Yet, Satan is always planning, always scheming to destroy the human soul at any cost. In this case, Satan is using something so common, so unique, and in many cases, innocent (as in the case of Harry Potter) to deceive an entire generation into a greater lie. That's his real, true nature, to bring about a deception that will be believed by many which will lead them into a far greater, deeper and more perverse lie, one which will cost them their soul.

It must be understood by all that by involving themselves in the occult, they are meddling with things of darkness. By associating themselves with the cares of this world, such as the case of horror films and those things which connect themselves to this genre, they are allowing demonic influences into their lives and they don't even know it. How many times have I received emails or letters by many who have found themselves lost in a world of the occult where they were being tormented and oppressed that they had no where to turn? The reason? Horror films. They allowed the subtle fantasy world of a writer or director to create a world that somehow seemed to appeal to the very nature of their own spirit, this in turn caused the individual to become lured into the very darkness Satan himself planned and designed. This would eventually bring bondage and in some situations, brought a demonic presence into their life.

Philippians 4:8 – "Finally, brethren, whatever is true, whatever is honorable, whatever is right, whatever is pure, whatever is lovely, whatever is of good repute, if there is any excellence and if anything worthy of praise, dwell on these things."

The Bible has plenty to say regarding the occult, sorcery, witchcraft and magic—we are to stay away from it (Deut. 18; 2 Kings 9; 2 Chron. 33:5-7; Micah 5:11-13; Nah. 3: 3-5; Gal. 5:19-21). In Acts 19, Paul visited Ephesus, which was a filthy city whose population practiced magic. Paul challenged them and instead of excusing away their behavior and getting angry with the message (and the messenger), many confessed their sin and burnt their magic books, so they could not practice again.

Ultimately, Christian participation in horror films is a matter of conscience before God. Whatever you choose, you must honor God by keeping yourself separate from the world and by showing mercy to those who are perishing. Horror films and the Christian faith are like oil and water, they cannot abide together in unity. It's message is one of hate, fear, seduction, manipulation, abuse, terror, fright and worry which brings forth bondage. The gospel is one of peace, joy, love, contentment, gladness and thanksgiving. When we look at both components we can clearly see that for the Christian, it is impossible to involve oneself with that which is unholy and spiritually perverse.

Making Evil look Good

Satan makes evil look good. While many in our culture today delight in blatant evil, Christians try to avoid evil. However, if it is disguised we can often be persuaded that it really isn't that bad. As an example, Mormonism, which has recently come into light because of the current political season, has created a clean image for itself, yet when we peer into the depths of

Mormonism, we realize the truth. Horror films follows suit, but the origins are full of darkness and evil.

From Aleister Crowley, L. Frank Baum, Bram Stoker or J. K. Rowling, the common denominator that bridges the gap between these people and those who have followed them is that they have tried to paint a picture which glorifies the occult to make it appealing to the unknowing victim. That is the power of seduction. From the first act in the garden, to a boy wizard, Satan has cleverly masquerades his design and his plans from the world, blinding many in his peddling of seductive poison. The only hope we have as believers is to be bold enough to remove the mask of his deception and reveal to the world why this world of monsters, ghouls and ghosts are not only wrong, but destructive.

If we are to manage this task given to us, then we must do all we can to be ready to expose the darkness that is building up all around us and stand firm in our uncompromising position that we, as believers, will not back down, we will not give in to the pressures of this world, but remain firm in our attempt to battle the evil which Satan has cast over this world. That is the only answer to evil, removing the mask and showing the world what is really going on.

"Therefore be imitators of God, as beloved children; and walk in love, just as Christ also loved you and gave Himself up for us, an offering and a sacrifice to God as a fragrant aroma. But immorality or any impurity or greed must not even be named among you, as is proper among saints; and there must be no filthiness and silly talk, or coarse jesting, which are not fitting, but rather giving of thanks. For this you know with certainty, that no immoral or impure person or covetous man, who is an idolater, has an inheritance in the kingdom of Christ and God. Let no one deceive you with empty words, for because of these things the wrath of God comes upon the sons of disobedience. Therefore do not be partakers with them; for you were formerly darkness, but now you are Light in the Lord; walk as children of Light (for the fruit of the Light consists in all goodness and righteousness and truth), trying to learn what is pleasing to the Lord. Do not participate in the unfruitful deeds of darkness, but instead even expose them; for it is disgraceful even to speak of the things which are done by them in secret. But all things become visible when they are exposed by the light, for everything that becomes visible is light."—Ephesians 5:1-13

Final Thoughts

So much hurting and loneliness in the world where people are cast from one extreme to the other, and the constant pulling away by deception all around us all makes our walk in this world hard at times. Still, even though we live in a world filled with mounting evil, there *is* hope.

There is no question that we live in a sin corrupted world, this is the nature of all things because of sin. But, just because there is sin, there is also Christ and what he did on the cross. Once we understand what the message the cross means, how that Christ came, born of a virgin, took upon himself the sins of the world, giving himself to die that we would not have to die eternally, died on a tree, yet rose again three days later, it gives us hope that even in this sin filled world, Christ makes a way out.

Yes, as I have shown throughout this book, there is great evil all around us, but what's important is how we respond to that evil. Do we participate in the things of the world because it may look appealing? Or do we distance ourselves so that we may walk clearer and holy, knowing that our walk is more important than those temporal things. It's not easy, it can be difficult at times, but that the reason why God gives us the Holy Spirit to guide us, to lead us and direct our paths.

The one thing I do see happening throughout this world, especially in the church is compromise. It seems as though many are not valuing their walk like they should and that bothers me greatly. The Apostle Paul tells us in 2 Timothy3:1-5 "This know also, that in the last days perilous times shall come. For men shall be lovers of their own selves, covetous, boasters, proud, blasphemers, disobedient to parents, unthankful, unholy. Without natural affection, truce breakers, false accusers, incontinent, fierce, despisers of those that are good, traitors, heady, high minded, lovers of pleasures more than lovers of God; having a form of godliness but denying its power. Have nothing to do with them."

When a Christian partakes of the occult world, irregardless of what that is, be it horror movies, books which promote Witchcraft and magic, or even music, especially heavy metal or Goth music, they are opening the door, literally giving permission to the enemy to have access to their life. The word tells us not to be conformed to this world, but be made new with the transformation of our mind to the cross, so that we can prove that which is good and acceptable and perfect will of God. (Romans 12:2) Sometimes this means literally walking away from those things which are harmful to ones spiritual growth.

I know that for me, it was this way when I was a fan of horror films. It took a sharp turn from watching anything even remotely connected to horror. Did it happen over night? Not at all. Yet, with God's grace and strength, the Holy Spirit literally helped me overcome that desire, and years later, that same strength has helped me overcome that need for entertainment.

That is the power and influence of the cross. No condemnation. No guilt. No pressure of failure. These are the traits of a loving and caring Father, not a hard taskmaster. All Christ asks of us is to place our complete trust and faith into him and what he did for us on the cross that is the answer - the cross.

If someone is struggling with things of the world, there is hope and that hope is found in the cross. When we come to Christ and allow him to transform our lives, he will. Yet, in order for that transformation to occur, there must be a willingness to submit to his perfect will. This is why it's hard for many for God to do what he wants in the lives of many, because they won't turn things over to him and just trust him. Faith doesn't come easy, faith is a hard road to walk, especially when there is uncertainty, yet, Abraham trusted God and he (God) counted it unto righteousness, his faith sustained him.

In this hour of great uncertainty, when we see things changing by the minute which used to seem as it would change by the year, we must do all we can to draw ourselves closer to the Lord. The enemy is slowly gaining complete dominance across the world, his dark shadow is spreading around the globe and we must be alert, swift to run and full of the spirit. These are the times in which we will see Biblical events unfold and now more than ever we must put away the things of this world and surrender all to Christ. Our soul literally depends on it.

Maybe you've come across this book and you *are* caught up in the world of Witchcraft or Satanism because of the deception Satan has sold you and you want out. There is hope and that hope is Jesus Christ. Only Christ can break the curse of sin and death and he broke it when he went to the cross for you and me. Satan's lie would tell you that all roads lead to God, yet that too is a lie. There is but one path to God and that is through his son, Jesus Christ. Witchcraft would tell you that powers and magic comes by the spirits, yet this too is a lie. Nothing comes for free, what Witchcraft offers is spiritual bondage, bondage to sin and death. The power those spirits promise are nothing more than temporary tricks, an illusion designed to draw you into a world of deceit.

Maybe you've become like others, gaining interest into ghosts and the paranormal. The truth is, while it might be at first exciting and new to entertain the idea one is communicating with the deceased - ghosts. The truth is, these are *not* ghosts, but demonic spirits. It must be understood that when we die in this life, it is then the judgment, and how you meet God is how you will be judged. Without Christ, without faith in him and accepting what he did on the cross, you are guilty under the law, it is that law which will condemn you to eternal damnation in a place called Hell. But there *is* hope.

God says in order to go to Heaven, you must be born again. In John 3:7, Jesus said to Nicodemus, "Ye must be born again." In the Bible God gives us the plan of how to be born again which means to be saved. His plan is simple! You can be saved today. How?

First, my friend, you must realize you are a sinner. "For all have sinned, and come short of the glory of God" (Romans 3:23). Because you are a sinner, you are condemned to death. "For the wages [payment] of sin is death" (Romans 6:23). This includes eternal separation from God in Hell. "It is appointed unto men once to die, but after this the judgment" (Hebrews 9:27).

But God loved you so much He gave His only begotten Son, Jesus, to bear your sin and die in your place. " . . . He hath made Him [Jesus, Who knew no sin] to be sin for us . . . that we might be made the righteousness of God in Him" (2 Corinthians 5:21).

Jesus had to shed His blood and die. "For the life of the flesh is in the blood" (Lev. 17:11). " . . . without shedding of blood is no remission [pardon]" (Hebrews 9:22).

" . . . God commendeth His love toward us, in that, while we were yet sinners, Christ died for us" (Romans 5:8).

Although we cannot understand how, God said my sins and your sins were laid upon Jesus and He died in our place. He became our substitute. It is true. God cannot lie.

Simply believe on Him as the one who bore your sin, died in your place, was buried, and whom God resurrected. His resurrection powerfully assures that the believer can claim everlasting life when Jesus is received as Savior. Surely, you realize you are a sinner. Right now, wherever you are, repenting, lift your heart to God in prayer.

In Luke 18:13, the sinner prayed: "God be merciful to me a sinner." Just pray: "Oh God, I know I am a sinner. I believe Jesus was my substitute when He died on the Cross. I believe His shed blood, death, burial, and resurrection were for me. I now receive Him as my Savior. I thank You for the forgiveness of my sins, the gift of salvation and everlasting life, because of Your merciful grace. Amen."

Just take God at His word and claim His salvation by faith. Believe, and you will be saved. No church, no lodge, no good works can save you. Remember, God does the saving. All of it!

God's simple plan of salvation is: You are a sinner. Therefore, unless you believe on Jesus Who died in your place, you will spend eternity in Hell. If you believe on Him as your crucified, buried, and risen Savior, you receive forgiveness for all of your sins and His gift of eternal salvation by faith. You say, "Surely, it cannot be that simple." Yes, that simple! It is scriptural. It is God's plan. My friend, believe on Jesus and receive Him as Savior today.

Horror Films might be fun and entertaining at first, but when the mask is pulled off, we finally see what Behind the Scream truly is - evil.

Printed in Great Britain
by Amazon.co.uk, Ltd.,
Marston Gate.